15 POSITIVE BEHAVIOR STRATEGIES TO INCREASE ACADEMIC SUCCESS

*To the memory of Eleanor Guetzloe, my dear colleague and friend,
who taught me the importance of hope, humor, and fun in teaching.*

*To family, especially Lonnie, and friends who are continual
sources of support and positive feedback.*

15 POSITIVE BEHAVIOR

STRATEGIES TO INCREASE ACADEMIC SUCCESS

Beverley Holden Johns

CORWIN
A SAGE Company

2455 Teller Road

Thousand Oaks, California 91320

(800) 233-9936

www.corwin.com

SAGE Publications Ltd.

1 Oliver's Yard

55 City Road

London EC1Y 1SP

United Kingdom

SAGE Publications India Pvt. Ltd.

B 1/I 1 Mohan Cooperative Industrial Area

Mathura Road, New Delhi 110 044

India

SAGE Publications Asia-Pacific Pte. Ltd.

3 Church Street

#10-04 Samsung Hub

Singapore 049483

Acquisitions Editor: Jessica Allan

Associate Editor: Kimberly Greenberg

Editorial Assistant: Cesar Reyes

Project Editor: Veronica Stapleton Hooper

Copy Editor: Pam Schroeder

Typesetter: C&M Digitals (P) Ltd.

Proofreader: Theresa Kay

Indexer: Sheila Bodell

Cover Designer: Glenn Vogel

Marketing Manager: Amanda Boudria

Copyright © 2015 by Corwin

All rights reserved. When forms and sample documents are included, their use is authorized only by educators, local school sites, and/or noncommercial or nonprofit entities that have purchased the book. Except for that usage, no part of this book may be reproduced or utilized in any form or by any means, electronic or mechanical, including photocopying, recording, or by any information storage and retrieval system, without permission in writing from the publisher.

All trade names and trademarks recited, referenced, or reflected herein are the property of their respective owners who retain all rights thereto.

Printed in the United States of America.

A catalog record of this book is available from the Library of Congress.

ISBN: 978-1-4833-4997-8

This book is printed on acid-free paper.

SFI Certified Sourcing
www.sfiprogram.org
SFI-00453

14 15 16 17 18 10 9 8 7 6 5 4 3 2 1

Contents

Acknowledgments

Corwin gratefully acknowledges the contributions of the following reviewers:

Sandra E. Archer
Peer Assistance and Review Teacher
Volusia County Schools, Ormond Beach, FL

Marsha Basanda
Fifth Grade Teacher
Monarch Elementary, Simpsonville, SC

Renee Bernhardt
Ed.S. Curriculum and Instruction, TSA for Learning Support
Cherokee County School District, Canton, GA

Mary Guerrette
Director of Special Education
MSAD #1, Presque Isle, ME

Mary Reeve, M.Ed.
Special Education Director
Gallup McKinley County Schools, NM

Sylvia Rockwell, Ph.D.
University Faculty
Saint Leo University, Palm Harbor, FL

Christine Ruder
Third Grade Teacher
Rolla Public Schools, Truman Elementary, MO

Joyce Sager, Ed.D.
Special Education Inclusion Teacher
Gadsden City Schools, AL

Susan E. Schipper
Teacher
Charles Street School, Palmyra BOE

Diane P. Smith
School Counselor
Smethport Area School District, PA

Rachel Spenner
Sixth Grade Literacy Teacher
Westridge Elementary, West Des Moines Community School District, IA

About the Author

 **Beverley Holden Johns** has 40 years of experience working with students with autism, learning disabilities (LD), and emotional and behavioral disorders (EBD) within the public schools. She supervised LD and EBD teachers in 22 school districts, was the founder and administrator of the Garrison Alternative School for students with severe EBD in Jacksonville, Illinois, and later the coordinator for staff development for the Four Rivers Special Education District. She is now a learning and behavior consultant, and a Professional Fellow at MacMurray College (where she teaches courses on Special Education Law, on Adaptations for the General Education Classroom, and on EBD). She chaired the 10th Biennial Conference of the International Association of Special Education (IASE) held June 10 to 14, 2007, in Hong Kong, served as President of IASE from 2006 until January 1, 2010, and presided over the 11th Biennial Conference in Alicante, Spain, in 2009. She presented the Inaugural Marden Lecture at The University of Hong Kong in January, 2006.

Johns is the lead author of 11 books (and coauthor of four others) including *401 Practical Adaptations for Every Classroom*; *Reduction of School Violence: Alternatives to Suspension* (4th edition); *Techniques for Managing Verbally and Physically Aggressive Students* (3rd edition); *Surviving Internal Politics Within the School*; *Safe Schools*; *Teacher's Reflective Calendar and Planning Journal*; *Special Educator's Reflective Calendar and Planning Journal*; *Effective Curriculum and Instruction for Students With Emotional/Behavioral Disorders*; *Students With Disabilities and General Education: A Desktop Reference for School Personnel*; *Getting Behavioral Interventions Right*; *Preparing Test-Resistant Students for Assessments: A Staff Training Guide*; *Ethical Dilemmas in Education*; *Motivating the Unmotivated Student*; *Reaching Students with Diverse Disabilities: Cross Categorical Ideas and Activities*; and *The Many Faces of Special Educators: Their Unique Talents in Working With Students With Special Needs*. She has written the workbook to accompany the video titled *Paraprofessional's Guide to Managing Student Behavior* and more than 40 education and special education articles.

She is coauthor with Janet Lerner of the seminal college LD textbook, the 13th edition of *Learning Disabilities and Related Disabilities*.

She developed an online course and appeared in a video for the Association of Supervision and Curriculum Development (ASCD) on the Common Core State Standards (CCSS) and students with disabilities.

She is the 2000 recipient of the Council for Exception Children (CEC) Outstanding Leadership Award from the International CEC, served for 3 years as Chair of CEC's Advocacy and Governmental Relations Committee, as past International President of the Council for Children With Behavioral Disorders (CCBD), and as past President of the CEC Pioneers, and received the 2007 Recipient of the Romaine P. Mackie Leadership Service Award.

She is listed in *Who's Who in the World, Who's Who in America, Who's Who of American Women, Who's Who in American Education,* and *Who's Who Among America's Teachers.* She has chaired the Illinois Special Education Coalition (ISELA; whose membership includes 14 statewide organizations) for 34 years.

She has presented workshops across the United States and Canada; in San Juan, Puerto Rico; Sydney, Australia (keynote); Warsaw, Poland; Wroclaw, Poland (keynote); Hong Kong; Lima, Peru; and Riga, Latvia.

She is the President of the Learning Disabilities Association (LDA) of Illinois and has been the National State Presidents' Representative on the Board of LDA of America.

She served as President of the Illinois Division on Learning Disabilities (DLD) and as Secretary and Governmental Relations Chair for the National Board of DLD.

She is a graduate of Catherine Spalding College in Louisville, Kentucky, and received a fellowship for her graduate work at Southern Illinois University (SIU) in Carbondale, where she received an M.S. in Special Education. She has done postgraduate work at the University of Illinois, Western Illinois University, SIU, and Eastern Illinois University.

Introduction

Behavior impacts academic success, and academic success or the lack of it impacts behavior. If students are successful in the classroom academically, there often can be a reduction in behavior problems. Acting out and work refusal impact academic success. Students may exhibit behavior problems because they require less effort or less embarrassment than to complete academic tasks.

Inappropriate behavior management and disruptions that result from inappropriate student behavior historically have contributed to school-related issues including reduced academic achievement (Alter, Walker, & Sanders, 2013).

This book focuses on evidence-based behavioral strategies that can be used to increase academic success. The relationship between problem behaviors and academic problems exhibited by students can be complex. Some students first exhibit academic difficulties with behavioral challenges such as aggression. They then receive little positive reinforcement, and the behavior problems increase. They don't progress in academics.

Others exhibit the aggression first, making them difficult to teach, and they fall behind. Students who exhibit aggressive behaviors are likely to develop negative relationships with teachers, and when problematic relationships exist between student and teacher, there is a likelihood of continued behavior and academic problems (Sutherland, Alder, & Gunter, 2003).

Approaches that work to improve classroom environments can enhance the likelihood that effective teaching and learning can occur, both for the students exhibiting problem behaviors and for the other students in the classroom (Epstein, Atkins, Cullinan, Kutash, & Weaver, 2008).

All teachers want to set their students up for academic success in positive ways. Behavior management strategies that are proactive and positive can make a difference in whether the student completes assignments, achieves at his or her level, and feels a sense of achievement every day in the classroom.

Educators want to know what behavior strategies actually work with specific students with challenging behaviors and how to implement those strategies so that students complete assignments and meet with academic success.

This book is designed for all educators as they strive to work with an increasing population of students who exhibit challenging behaviors and work to ensure that their students are academically successful at a time when academic performance is foremost in the public eye. Drawing upon research and my many years of experience in working with students with significant behavioral challenges, this book focuses on 15 evidence-based behavior management strategies and how to implement those strategies in the academic tasks that are expected of students.

Many times if we reframe how academic tasks are presented, students are more likely to complete the task successfully. We know there is a relationship between academic tasks and behavior and we need to utilize what we know about behavior to provide academic tasks that result in achievement.

There are 15 different short chapters with each one focusing on a specific positive behavior management strategy and how that strategy or set of strategies can be used in academic tasks. Some examples are provided for applying the strategies to the Common Core State Standards (CCSS).

Each chapter opens with the definition of the strategy and then provides two case scenarios that depict the actual strategy in action—live action from the classroom. One case shows how the strategy is used at the elementary level, and one shows how the strategy is used at the secondary level. Some of the examples incorporate how the strategies can be implemented with the CCSS.

With the focus on the use of evidence-based interventions, the research that supports the use of each technique is provided so that you can delve more into any chosen topic.

Each strategy provides key points to remember in implementation and how to implement with fidelity. Helpful suggestions for involving parents in the interventions are provided, too.

We want our parents to be our allies, and parents know their children best, so we must seek their input before we utilize interventions. We need to explain those interventions to parents and why we are utilizing them. We can also build a number of these interventions into homework assignments.

The importance of collaboration with other educators is stressed. In today's schools, our students see multiple individuals throughout the day, and we need to work together with those individuals to create a coordinated plan. We never have all the answers and need to work with others when we are determining which of these strategies will work with specific students.

In this era of accountability, we must show that what we are doing is effective with our students, so it is critical that we keep data. Recognizing the challenge of having time to get everything done during the day, this book provides simple ways to collect data to show whether an intervention is successful with a student.

There are also sections that focus on troubleshooting when an intervention isn't working. We may attempt to use an intervention because we have heard that it is effective only to find that the intervention didn't work. The troubleshooting advice assists you in determining what may have gone wrong.

The last section in each chapter is a quick checklist to assist the reader in remembering the key components of the intervention.

Throughout the chapters, there are charts and sample activities that you can utilize.

The book provides a tool kit that you can use when determining what to do when you are faced with students with challenging behaviors who are not achieving successfully. As you become familiar with the strategies, you can match the needs of the individual student or students with the strategy that might be most effective. One intervention will not work with all students, but among the 15, you will be able to get a better picture of what might work best. You will also note that some interventions can be used together with other interventions.

Read on to become familiar with a variety of behavior management strategies that will help your students achieve academically.

Strategy 1

Attributions

The Power of Attributing
Student Success to Efforts

ATTRIBUTIONS DEFINED

Attributions refer to one's beliefs concerning the outcomes of one's actions. Attributions are our perceptions about the causes of our success and failure (Weiner, 2005). Stable attributions are those that refer to an individual's personal attributes—internal attributions. External attributions refer to forces external to the individual. Within internal attributions there are stable attributions—those about ability—and there are those that are seen as temporal—dealing with the person's efforts. Attributions that are seen as stable are believed to be less alterable than are temporal attributions. It is best to attribute success to internal temporal factors such as effort. Bad outcomes should be interpreted as alterable (Bryan, 1998).

Attributions are individuals' explanatory beliefs about why things happen to them. Teachers must stress accurate, facilitative attributions throughout the day and to teach their students to do the same. Facilitative attributions associate student success with controllable factors such as effort, the correct use of strategies, and persistence. Facilitative attributions are statements that the student was successful because he or she stuck to it or followed a cue card or tried very hard (Margolis & McCabe, 2003).

LIVE ACTION FROM THE CLASSROOM

"I hate math, and you can't make me do it. Math is just too hard, and I'm stupid in it." The words come out of Jason's mouth during the first week of school.

Mr. Sands is a fourth grade teacher and prides himself on how well he teaches mathematics and reading and how well he motivates his students in math. This year, Jason is in his class, and Mr. Sands is frustrated with Jason's comments about his own stupidity and his hatred toward math. He wants to instill in Jason a sense that, if Jason works hard at his math, he can do well.

Mr. Sands decides that he will work with Jason on his math. He reviews Jason's records and finds that Jason is achieving at a third grade level in math. He knows he will have to work hard to give Jason work at his achievement level and work to build his skills—actually, 10 other students in his class are achieving at approximately the same level.

Mr. Sands provides Jason with math problems—he uses concrete objects to show how to do the problems, and he provides step-by-step directions and many examples. He starts out with a few problems for Jason to do at one time. When Jason completes those, Mr. Sands praises him and says, "Jason, you worked hard at that—your efforts really paid off." Jason is pleased with himself.

Mr. Sands slowly increases the number of math problems that Jason does—frequently praising Jason and attributing Jason's success to his own efforts. Jason becomes more confident in his math skills and beams when Mr. Sands praises his efforts. Jason has gained more confidence in his ability.

Within 3 months, Mr. Sands notices that Jason is helping other students with their math. Mr. Sands has to chuckle to himself because one day he overhears Jason talking to another student and praising that student— attributing the other student's success to his efforts and hard work. By the end of the year, Jason has made significant progress and is at grade level. Furthermore, Jason likes math.

Read on to see how this strategy is used at the secondary level. Mrs. Ebert has a young lady, Carrie Ann, in her high school English class. Mrs. Ebert is really impressed with Carrie Ann's writing talent. She is very creative when she does write. However, Mrs. Ebert has a great deal of difficulty getting Carrie Ann to write. Carrie Ann only completes her assignments about 50 percent of the time. Mrs. Ebert talks to Carrie about what is going on. She shares with Carrie that she is really impressed with her writing talent. Carrie Ann says the stories that she did turn in were just luck and she really doesn't have any talent at all.

Mrs. Ebert explains to Carrie that she would like to help Carrie develop her talent, but she needs Carrie to try. In class the next day, Mrs. Ebert gives a creative writing assignment about a topic that she knows Carrie is interested in. Carrie has told her she wants to be a fashion designer, so the assignment is for students to write about a fashion trend they have observed. She tells the students they have to write at least three paragraphs. Because the assignment is short and is about an interest of Carrie's, Carrie completes the assignment and receives an A. Mrs. Ebert tells Carrie that she did well because she put forth the effort, and she explains to Carrie that she knows she will continue to put forth the effort.

In the case of Carrie, Mrs. Ebert knew it was important to ensure Carrie's success and then to attribute Carrie's success to her effort.

WHAT THE RESEARCH SAYS

There is a body of research that says that students who are able to attribute their success to their role or effort make better academic and behavioral progress than those students who attribute their success to outside forces.

When students attributed their successful school performance to personal, controllable causes such as effort, they enhance their work and increase the probability of their success. In one study, hope was found to have direct and indirect impact through attributions on successful school performance (Stephanou, 2012).

In a study in 2011 with African American adolescents, it was found that boys were more likely than girls to attribute math successes to high ability and to attribute English failures to low ability. When students believed that their failure was due to low ability, students may be less persistent and may believe that their low ability will limit the positive effects of effort on their part (Swinton, Kurtz-Costes, Rowley, & Okeke-Adeyanju, 2011).

Attributing task failure to one's abilities can result in maladaptive outcomes because ability is considered a stable causal factor that students are unable to control. In one study, individuals knew that attributing their success to ability was maladaptive, but they couldn't avoid engaging in such attributions (Sakaki & Murayama, 2013).

In an early study by Okolo in 1992, computer-assisted instruction was utilized with attribution versus neutral feedback for students learning multiplication facts. Ability attribution feedback was given to the students after each set of five problems—statements such as "You really know these" (p. 329) and effort feedback such as "You are really trying hard or "You can get it if you keep trying" (p. 329). Students in the attribution training group made significant improvements in multiplication performance compared to the students who received neutral feedback (Okolo, 1992).

Bryan (1998) found that students with learning disabilities are more internal in their attributions for their failure but are less likely than their normal-achieving peers to be internal in their attributions for success. In other words, if these children are successful, they attribute it to someone being nice to them or the work being easy. When they do badly, they attribute it to the fact that they are not smart. Students without learning disabilities tend to attribute failure to lack of effort (Hallahan, Gajar, Cohne, & Tarver, 1978).

Attributions are best if the teacher gives the student the appropriate conditions for students to learn—conditions under which the child's efforts pay off. This includes being sure that the work is at the correct level of difficulty, teachers must be ready to give help when the student needs it, and teachers must remember that ability can change incrementally (Weiner, 2005). Increases in ability have happened in part because of effort.

What is the impact of attributions on behavior? In a study by Anderson, Horowitz, and French (1983), it was found that children and adults who were lonely attributed their social success to external and unstable causes and their social failure to internal and stable causes.

When students attribute their behavior problems to hostile intent toward peers, there is a strong association with aggressive behavior (Lambert & Miller, 2010).

Bryan (1998) found that, rather than spending time building student self-concept, educators should focus their efforts on teaching students to attribute their success to their efforts.

Another study measured how teachers' feedback impacted student performance. Stipek and Daniels (1988) found that teachers' feedback did impact the performance of kindergarten children. In classes where normative evaluations were given such as graded assignments, best papers placed on bulletin boards, or positive or negative feedback after tests, those children rated their competence lower than those children in classes where normative evaluation was not emphasized. In those classes, comments as opposed to grades were given on assignments and on report cards, comparisons with others were discouraged, and children were encouraged to seek help from their classmates.

Examples and non-examples of attribution statements

Examples	Non-examples
You did well because you worked hard.	You did OK because I taught you well.
You listened carefully, and it paid off.	Jenny helped you with the key points of the lecture.
It is apparent that you studied and read a great deal of information about the Vietnam War.	I am glad I provided you with the notes you needed to learn about the war.
You showed a lot of effort on this assignment.	That work was really easy.

BASIC DIRECTIONS TO FOLLOW WHEN UTILIZING THIS INTERVENTION

Educators should always attribute student performance to those factors that are within the child's control (Association for Supervision and Curriculum Development, 2013). When students succeed, it is important to accentuate what the student did that achieved his or her success. As an example, if students did well on a math test, the success should be attributed to the fact that they really put forth a great deal of effort or studied hard or used the skills that they had learned.

1. Assess the student's level in the particular academic task to determine whether you are providing assignments that are at the appropriate instructional level.

2. Engage the student in an academic task at the appropriate instructional level.

3. Give the student interpretive feedback about the causes of performance—"You have really been working hard" or "All your effort on this task has really made a difference."

4. Encourage the student to make the same interpretation. Make sure that the student makes statements that attribute success to his or her efforts. Agree and reinforce the student when he or she makes attribution statements.

5. Model the use of attribution statements when you are completing a task that the student observes; for example, "I am so glad you enjoyed doing our geography lesson. I really worked hard to plan it for you. It was sure worth my effort to see all of you do so well."

6. Give yourself credit for matching the students' performance level with the work you give to the students.

7. When collecting data, you will want to collect it both on how you use attribution statements with your students and also on how your students use attribution statements about their own efforts. To monitor your use of attribution statements, you can simply keep a tally sheet on your desk or in your pocket and mark down how many times you make statements that attribute the success of your students to their efforts. Look at your tally sheet at the end of the day to see how you have done and vow that you will increase the statements the next day. Remember that, when we are modeling the use of those statements, we are showing students how they can use such statements.

When collecting data on how your students use attribution statements, you can keep a sticky note on each student's desk or a small sheet of paper with the name of each day of the week on each student's desk. Each time you hear the student make a statement about how his or her success is attributed to effort, you can place a mark on the sheet, and either at the end of the day or the end of the week, you can review it with individual students and keep the data on how they are doing on its use. Remember that it will be important that you have taught your students how to use the statements and provided them with examples.

Working With Parents to Promote the Use of Attribution Statements

When working with parents and establishing a positive rapport, use attribution statements with them as well as with the students.

"I admire your efforts in getting your child to school every day."

"The help you gave your child with his homework really made a difference in his grade. I appreciate your effort."

"You really worked hard to get to this conference."

These are examples of attribution statements you can make to parents. Praise their efforts to cooperate with you to achieve success for their child. By modeling such statements, the parents learn how to use the comments at home with their child.

Stress with parents how they can use attribution statements with their child when they are helping the child with homework. You can suggest that the parents praise the child when the child is working hard on his or her homework by saying, "You are really working hard on that homework. I am so proud of your efforts."

When you write notes home to the parents, use attribution statements about the child: "Bill really put forth the effort on his math today and got an A on the assignment" or "Jim stuck with his science project until he got it done."

Troubleshooting if the Intervention Is Not Working

1. The work I am giving may be too difficult for the child and is so frustrating that the child is unable to achieve success. The child then sees that, even if he or she tries, he or she is unable to complete the task.

2. Other students may be putting the student down, and I am not hearing their comments. They may be sabotaging the success of the student. It is critical that I listen for such negative comments and not allow those. I need to continually encourage each student's efforts.

3. In the process of providing attributions to one student, I may be forgetting to use these statements with all of my students.

4. I need to consider whether I am matching the work I am giving the student with the specific needs of the student—visual, auditory, tactile, kinesthetic.

A Checklist to Help You Remember

✓ Do I tune in to what my students are saying about why they succeed or don't succeed?

✓ Do I frequently tell my students that their success is due to their efforts?

✓ Do I chart my positive attribution statements to my students to see if I am increasing my use?

✓ Do I model the use of attributions by attributing my good work to my effort?

✓ Do I reinforce my students verbally when I hear them attributing their success to their effort?

✓ Do I understand that the student may have been in the habit of attributing success or lack of it to outside forces and it may take a period of time to change the behavior?

Strategy 2

Behavior Momentum

Beginning With Easy Tasks That Ensure Success in More Difficult Tasks

BEHAVIOR MOMENTUM DEFINED

Behavior momentum is defined as the utilization of a series of preferred behaviors to increase the probability that non-preferred behaviors will occur (Lee, Belfiore, & Budin, 2008). A series of brief preferred tasks that are likely to result in compliance are presented just prior to tasks with a low probability of compliance. The student gains momentum for success and completes the difficult task.

The intervention is more effective when educators deliver praise after the compliance of the high-probability or preferred tasks (Lee, 2005).

The teacher must identify the high-probability tasks and requests—they should be short in duration, requiring less than 5 seconds to complete, and have a success history for the student. The teacher should arrange two to three high-probability task sequences prior to each low-probability task. For verbal requests, deliver a series of two to four high-probability requests immediately before the low-probability task.

LIVE ACTION FROM THE CLASSROOM

Mrs. Holden, a third grade teacher, is worried. She has to give Marilee one of the state tests today and tomorrow. Marilee missed the test last week. Mrs. Holden has the feeling that Marilee didn't come to school last week because she didn't want to take the test. Marilee is struggling with her schoolwork this year, partly because of attendance issues and problems that are occurring within the home.

Mrs. Holden wants to make sure that Marilee does as well as she can on the test. Marilee is a good reader but struggles with math skills. She is very anxious about taking tests. Frankly, Mrs. Holden is afraid that Marilee will shut down and refuse to take the test.

Mrs. Holden has used behavior momentum many times during this school year and knows that she better use the technique for this potentially difficult situation. The administrator has hired a substitute for Mrs. Holden, so she is able to administer the test privately to Marilee. She has no other students who have to take the state test as a makeup.

Mrs. Holden determines that she must plan three tasks that have a high probability for Marilee's success prior to the time she administers the test. Mrs. Holden has prepared a matching game with possible test direction words on some cards and their meanings on other cards. There are a total of three words and three meanings. Prior to taking the test, Mrs. Holden asks Marilee to read the test direction words quickly—Marilee does so very easily, and Mrs. Holden verbally praises her for her efforts. Mrs. Holden then asks Marilee to read the cards with the meanings on them. Marilee again does so easily and is beginning to become more comfortable, so she smiles. Mrs. Holden lets her know that her effort is really paying off. Mrs. Holden then shuffles the cards quickly and puts the cards facedown, and Marilee has to match the cards with the directions. Marilee does so easily, is very pleased, and is praised by Mrs. Holden. Mrs. Holden then provides Marilee the test, and Marilee, feeling much more confident, begins.

At the secondary level, Mrs. Ingles is a high school math teacher teaching Algebra II. She has noticed that one of her students, Jacob, has really hit a roadblock and is having a great deal of difficulty even though he excelled in Algebra I. Mrs. Ingles is very concerned. She has noted that Jacob is having difficulty grasping the concepts, and the more difficulty he has in grasping the concepts, the more frustrated he becomes. He is having a high degree of anxiety because of the frustration and is now showing signs that he is ready to give up.

Mrs. Ingles believes he can grasp the concepts, but now his anxiety is really interfering. She decides she is going to use behavior momentum with Jacob. She explains the concepts to the entire class using both auditory and visual cues. If she sees that Jacob is looking confused, she uses it as an opportunity to reteach the concept to the entire class because she believes that there are probably other students who may be having difficulty understanding it, too.

Mrs. Ingles completely rewrites her practice worksheets that are given to some of the students. She passes the worksheets out so students don't know who is getting which worksheets. For those students who are having difficulty understanding the concepts and for Jacob, she starts each worksheet with three easy Algebra I problems. She moves around the room helping students as needed. When she gets to Jacob and other students who are struggling and sees that they are able to get the first problem done, she comments to them personally, "Way to go. You've got it. Keep up the good work." When she sees him get the next one right, she again makes a positive comment to Jacob about the effort he is making. She does that again when he gets the third one completed. Mrs. Ingles finds now that Jacob is gaining confidence and then he tries the next problem, which is an Algebra II problem. Mrs. Ingles has built momentum for Jacob's success.

WHAT THE RESEARCH SAYS

Vostal and Lee (2011) studied behavior momentum with adolescents with emotional and behavioral disorders during a specific continuous reading task. They found that, when students read a third grade level paragraph immediately before they read the fifth grade paragraph, the results showed that students were able to increase the number of words correctly on the first 10 words of the fifth grade paragraph.

In a study conducted by Burns and colleagues (2009) fourth grade students were asked to read 100 sixth grade words and first grade words. In the behavior momentum group, the students were asked to read the 20 first grade words prior to the entire list of 100 sixth grade words. Students read the 100 sixth grade words with significantly greater fluency than the students in the control group. The students could read the first grade words easily and then continued to read the sixth grade words at a rapid pace because they had built up the momentum for fluency.

Ducharme and Worling (1994) used the technique for children with developmental disabilities and found behavior momentum to be effective. They then began to reduce or fade the high-probability requests that preceded the low-probability requests. They dropped the fun requests from three to two, then from two to one. Then they delayed the time between the high-probability request and the low-probability request. As an example, they said "Pick up your toys" and waited 10 seconds rather than immediately.

Lee and colleagues (2006) also found that the latency or the time lag from high-probability to low-probability tasks was shorter than the latency from low-probability to subsequent high-probability tasks. And they recommended that the low-probability tasks be delivered within 10 seconds of the high-probability tasks.

Mace, Auro, Oyajian, and Ckert (1997) found that the effectiveness of behavioral momentum was increased with the quality of the reinforcers of the high-probability requests. The reinforcement must be considered very desirable for the student.

BASIC DIRECTIONS TO FOLLOW WHEN UTILIZING THIS INTERVENTION

Behavior momentum is an effective strategy to utilize when students are resistant to specific academic tasks. In order for the teacher to use it successfully, the teacher must know which tasks are easy for the student to do and which tasks will present challenges.

1. Determine specific tasks of a short duration that you know the student can complete successfully. Begin by providing three of those tasks one right after the other to the student. When the student is successful with each of those tasks, he or she should be praised for completing each task.

2. When the student has completed the tasks that are of a high probability of success, you should then give the student the more difficult task. When the student starts the task, you should reinforce the child. It is important for you to monitor the student as he or she approaches the difficult task because you can then praise the student for making the effort to begin.

3. When the student completes the more difficult task, you should reinforce the student.

4. When this technique becomes effective for the child when three tasks are provided that have a high probability for success, you can then reduce the number of tasks that have a high probability for success down to two. After a period of time when behavioral change has occurred, you can reduce the high-probability task to one preceding the more difficult task.

5. Offer self-reinforcement for your perception of the student's need for serial success and your ability to lay the groundwork for the student to proceed with more challenging material.

6. Keep data to ensure that the procedure is working according to plan. Lee and colleagues (2008) recommend that you collect data on two

Figure 2.1 Behavior Momentum

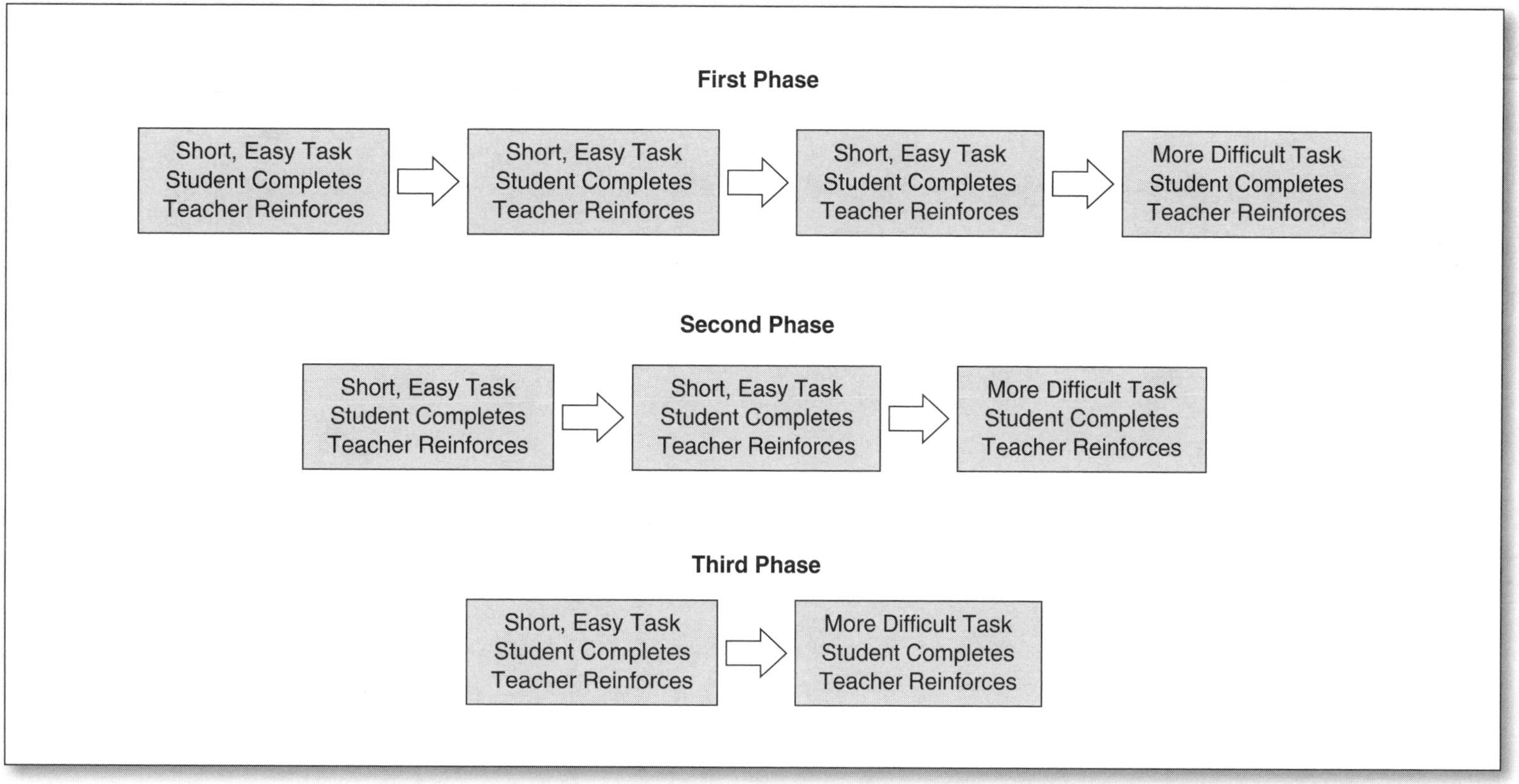

First Phase

Short, Easy Task	Short, Easy Task	Short, Easy Task
Student Completes	Student Completes	Student Completes
Teacher Reinforces	Teacher Reinforces	Teacher Reinforces

Short, Easy Task / Student Completes / Teacher Reinforces → Short, Easy Task / Student Completes / Teacher Reinforces → Short, Easy Task / Student Completes / Teacher Reinforces → More Difficult Task / Student Completes / Teacher Reinforces

Second Phase

Short, Easy Task / Student Completes / Teacher Reinforces → Short, Easy Task / Student Completes / Teacher Reinforces → More Difficult Task / Student Completes / Teacher Reinforces

Third Phase

Short, Easy Task / Student Completes / Teacher Reinforces → More Difficult Task / Student Completes / Teacher Reinforces behaviors when using behavior momentum. For verbal requests, collect data on the percentage of low-probability requests completed. For written work, document the number of low-probability math problems or words performed successfully. You can see first-hand the progress the student is making. Also collect data on high-probability requests, meaning at which level the student does math problems easily or at which level the student reads words easily.

Working With Parents on the Use of Behavior Momentum

When working with parents, explain your use of behavior momentum within the classroom. Provide examples of how the parent may want to utilize behavior momentum for chores or tasks at home. As an example, when the parent wants the child to clean his or her room, the parent can request that the student turn off the light in the bathroom or hang up the towel or turn down the television. These are just some examples of tasks that the child could do easily. Then the parent can request that the child put his or her shoes in the closet—the non-preferred activity. To provide parents with high-probability items for the parent to use, ask the parents about an easy task that they know their child can do with no difficulty. Then ask the parents what the desired behavior is they wish to achieve, and explain that the easy tasks should be given before the more difficult task.

You can also strive to incorporate behavior momentum in homework assignments that are provided. You can provide three easy math problems or a very easy reading assignment prior to giving the more difficult math problems or the more difficult reading assignments.

You can also utilize behavior momentum when asking for parents to volunteer to do certain tasks needed for the classroom. You can provide some easy tasks that you know will require very little effort on the part of the parents. You then let the parents know how much their efforts are appreciated. Then when you want the parents to volunteer for a more difficult task like speaking to the class about their occupation or accompanying the class on a field trip, the parent is more likely to volunteer.

Troubleshooting if the Intervention Is Not Working

1. The reinforcement I am giving to the student when the student has successfully completed the high-probability tasks and the low-probability requests may not really be reinforcing to the student. Am I sure that my comments to the student are sincere and genuine?

2. The difficult task I am providing to the student may be beyond the realm of possibility of completion by the student.

3. The high-probability tasks may not really be such and may not be easy enough for the student to complete.

4. I may not be providing enough high-probability tasks prior to the low probability of success task.

5. I may need to find a task that closely resembles a previously successful task with the exception of a very minor feature.

A Checklist to Help You Remember

✓ Do I build the momentum for success by providing tasks that are easy for the students prior to giving the students a task that might be challenging for them?

✓ Do I identify tasks that are quick and easy for the student to complete and will in all probability result in compliance?

✓ Do I understand that children must believe that they can complete tasks successfully in order to tackle more difficult tasks?

✓ Do I know the specific levels of my students, so I am able to determine which tasks may be easy versus which ones may be difficult for them? Have I thoroughly assessed my students to determine those levels?

Strategy 3

Behavior Interspersal

*Interspersing Easy Tasks
With Difficult Tasks*

BEHAVIOR INTERSPERSAL DEFINED

Behavior interspersal is the process of mixing within assignments an assignment or assignments that are briefer or easier than others. If you are providing a set of assignments for students to complete, you intersperse assignments that are likely to result in student success. These assignments will be ones that you know the student is able to do independently without assistance and will result in a sense of accomplishment for the student. The assignment provides a short break for a student who is engaging in a series of assignments. I have heard a teacher refer to this as *behavior sandwiching* because you are mixing difficult assignments with easy assignments.

LIVE ACTION FROM THE CLASSROOM

Look at how Mr. Boston utilized behavior interspersal with his third graders. At least three of Mr. Boston's students do not like math and often refuse to do it. The three students are doing math independently at the second grade level. Mr. Boston decided to redesign his math worksheets for these students. He starts each sheet with three third grade problems. Each time he sees one of the students complete a math problem at the third grade level, he moves to the student's desk and praises him or her. He then intersperses three first grade level math problems before returning to two or three third grade problems and then goes to each student to provide assistance on the third grade problems. He then starts replacing the first grade level problems with second grade level problems and intersperses those with the third grade problems.

In the other third grade class taught by Mrs. Carr, there are about seven of the 25 students who are struggling with math. Even though test scores show that they should be able to do third grade math work, they can't or won't do it when it involves doing independent math worksheets. Some of them will do two problems and then quit, some of them won't start at all, and some rush through and put down any answer, which in most cases is wrong. Mrs. Carr is frustrated because she believes they can do the math but not in the way it is presented. She looks over the types of worksheets she is using and decides that she will adapt them by using behavior interspersal. She has decided she will combine behavior interspersal with behavior momentum. She prepares new worksheets for the students. She puts three easy math problems first; they are at the first and second grade levels.

She then puts two third grade level math problems right after the easy ones. Next are two more easy first and second grade math problems and then three third grade level math problems. Then she adds two more easy ones and three third grade level problems. She provides the whole class with their math worksheets but provides different ones to the students who are struggling. She calls no attention to the fact that the math worksheets are different. After she has disseminated the math worksheets, she then utilizes proximity control. She moves around the room, and when she sees that the individual students have done the first three problems, she reinforces them. She then notes that they are actually attempting the grade level problems and are being successful in completing them. She continues to move around the room, reinforcing the students for staying on task and completing the math problems. She notices that the students are completing the math worksheets for the first time. She decides that she will continue this approach and will gradually increase the number of difficult problems that are expected by having the students do two easy ones followed by four difficult ones. She will monitor this system to determine when she should fade it out more. Both Mr. Boston and Mrs. Carr are so pleased that behavior interspersal has really made the difference in getting the students to complete their math problems.

Mr. Atkins has Rachel in his last-period high school English literature class. Rachel has a significant learning disability in the area of written expression and often comes into class looking very tired. She goes to her seat and puts her head down on her desk. Mr. Atkins is concerned that she doesn't want to do any work, but he does not want to make this assumption without doing some further exploration. Rachel sees a special education resource teacher, and Mr. Atkins talks with the resource teacher, who shares that Rachel is working very hard in her other classes and she believes that Rachel is tired by the end of the day from giving everything she has to her tasks. Mr. Atkins collaborates with the special education teacher to determine how to help Rachel during this last-period class.

They decide that Mr. Atkins will use a behavior interspersal technique with Rachel. Based on his observations and her participation in class, he knows that Rachel likes to read and discuss the literature, but a significant portion of the class period is devoted to answering questions in writing about the specific literature assignment. Each day, Mr. Atkins briefly discusses the literature assignment, and Rachel pays attention, but then the remainder of the class period is spent with the students individually writing answers to a set of questions provided. Rachel finds this very difficult because she is tired of writing by the end of the day.

Mr. Atkins examines the structure that he is using in class because he has other students who seem unmotivated during the class period.

He decides to begin class with a short lecture (5–7 minutes) about the specific literature assignment. He will then ask the students one question and has them discuss it verbally in a small group, asking Rachel to lead her small group. Next, he will ask the students another question about the content and have each student write down the answer. He will then lecture a short amount of time again and ask the students to verbally discuss a question. For the next question, he will have the students write down the answer.

Rachel does very well listening to the short 5-minute lectures and does well leading a group in a verbal discussion, but writing down answers is difficult, so Mr. Atkins is interspersing two easy tasks for Rachel with one difficult task, which is writing down an answer. He is interspersing easy with hard, and as a result, he finds that Rachel is beginning to respond better and is actually working to write down her answers. Mr. Atkins is also utilizing behavior momentum by beginning the class with two easy tasks and then introducing the difficult task. Then he keeps interspersing easy tasks with the difficult ones until the class period is over. Mr. Atkins also allows Rachel to use a word processing tool.

Mr. Atkins finds that many of his other students are also enjoying this format.

WHAT THE RESEARCH SAYS

In a study with students with emotional and behavioral disorders, students were given a choice of homework grammar assignments with brief, discrete interspersed paragraphs or those without those paragraphs. Students preferred the assignments with brief, additional interspersed discrete tasks, and the assignment alteration method increased the likelihood that the student would complete the task (Teeple & Skinner, 2004).

Because students show a preference for assignments that are briefer or easier, interspersing those types of tasks with more difficult tasks may be an efficient way to increase the probability that students will choose to work independently and the technique may improve perceptions of learning (Skinner et al., 1999). Interspersing additional brief problems in mathematics can increase problem completion rates and the probability of students choosing an assignment with additional brief tasks (McCurdy, Skinner, Grantham, Watson, & Hindman, 2001; Skinner, 2002).

In a study completed by McCurdy and colleagues (2001), it was found that, for a fourth grade student with behavior problems, if brief items were interspersed with regular items on a math seatwork assignment, the results showed that there was more on-task behavior than if the student just completed the regular seatwork assignment.

Burns and colleagues (2009) conducted a study with fourth graders in which interspersal and behavioral momentum were utilized in reading. Participants were to read either a behavioral momentum, interspersed, or controlled word list. Twenty first grade words were interspersed among 100 sixth grade words. After every fifth word at the sixth grade level was a first grade word. The results of the study showed that the interspersal conditions didn't result in change of behavior in reading unless they involved high levels of reinforcement for reading the easier words as well as the harder words. The researchers noted that there may not have been enough easy items used.

Figure 3.1   Behavior Interspersal Flowchart

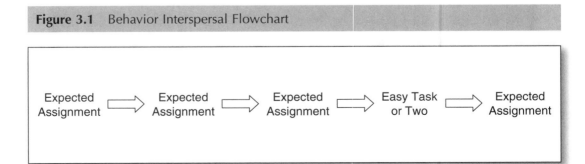

BASIC DIRECTIONS TO FOLLOW WHEN UTILIZING THIS INTERVENTION

Behavior interspersal is an excellent intervention that gives a student a break from doing a series of difficult tasks by interspersing easy tasks throughout the assignment.

1. Through a variety of assessment tools, determine at which level work is easy for the student and at which level work is too difficult for the student. It is critical that you understand the strengths and weaknesses of the student so that you are able to determine what an appropriate easy task is for the student so that the easy task can be interspersed with difficult ones. By working together with the special education resource teacher, Mr. Atkins confirmed that Rachel had a significant problem in written expression, and that was what the majority of his class assignments were. He also learned that Rachel liked English literature and enjoyed short lectures, and she liked to lead verbal discussions. As a result, he knew that the interspersed activities needed to be those that involved Rachel listening to a short lecture and leading a small group in an oral discussion.

2. Mr. Boston knew the students' math levels and designed math worksheets with easy math problems interspersed with more difficult problems.

3. Thoroughly plan how you will intersperse the difficult work with the easy work.

4. Consider using behavior interspersal together with behavior momentum. Mr. Atkins began to build momentum by giving a short lecture and then having a short oral discussion where Rachel could lead her discussion group. He then gave the difficult assignment of writing down one answer. He kept interspersing easy tasks with the written assignment. This is, however, optional. You don't have to use the two together because they are two separate interventions.

5. When utilizing this intervention, it is important to know the attention spans of the students within the class. Mr. Atkins knew that he was having difficulty with many of the students being motivated, so he knew he had to do shorter assignments with the students to hold their attention.

As Mr. Atkins got more comfortable with this new format he was using, he started bringing in multiple other activities to reinforce his lectures including short YouTube videos about what was being discussed, bringing in pictures of some of the characters, and even dressing up as one of the characters.

6. Behavior interspersal is most effective when students are reinforced for completing both the easy sections of the task as well as the more difficult parts of the task.

7. When collecting data on behavior interspersal, chart how many tasks in each subject a student is able to do before you see the first signs of frustration. This then gives you an idea about when you need to intersperse an easy activity or two. It is important to keep a record of the student's ability to stay on a task. I recommend that you utilize interspersal for a subject area where you note that the student is engaging in avoidance behavior or is struggling with the subject. This data should be very useful to future teachers, and it gives you an opportunity to see whether the completion rates of the students increase.

Working With Parents on the Use of Behavior Interspersal

When holding conferences with parents, show them how you are utilizing behavior interspersal with the students within your classroom. Discuss how it gives the students a break from the more difficult work that is expected of them. Provide ideas for parents about how they can utilize this strategy at home. When they are expecting their child to do chores at home, they may want to provide two to three chores, then give the child a very easy, short job to do to give the child a break, and then return to the more difficult task.

Utilize behavior interspersal when you provide homework assignments to students. As an example, in math, you may want to give the student an assignment that is at their grade level and, because it is homework, that you know they can do independently. After three problems, intersperse one to two problems that are below the student's achievement level, then return to the homework at the student's grade level.

Troubleshooting if the Intervention Is Not Working

1. One of the most likely problems that can occur is that the work that I have determined to be easy or the work that I have determined to be at the appropriate level is in fact not at the appropriate level.

2. I may not be providing enough behavior-specific praise for correct answers for the easy tasks and the difficult tasks.

3. I may be providing too many difficult questions or problems before I intersperse an easy one.

A Checklist to Help You Remember

✓ Do I know the specific level of the student so that the tasks I use to intersperse are likely to result in the student's success?

✓ Do I know the length of the attention span of the student in order to determine how frequently to intersperse the briefer or easier task?

✓ Do I reinforce the student while the student is engaging in task completion?

✓ Do I utilize behavior interspersal together with behavior momentum when possible?

Strategy 4

Behavior-Specific Praise

Letting Students Know Exactly What They Did When You Reinforce Them

BEHAVIOR-SPECIFIC PRAISE DEFINED

Behavior-specific praise refers to the practice where the teacher recognizes the student for engaging in appropriate behavior and tells the students exactly what the behavior was that the teacher liked. Positive attention is most effective when it is immediate and when it is specific. Statements like, "Thank you for raising your hand," "You were a big help to Donny with his math problem," and "Thank you for walking in the hall" are behavior-specific praise statements.

Comments such as, "Way to go," "Good job," or "Nice" are generalized praise statements that can leave the student wondering what he or she did correctly.

LIVE ACTION FROM THE CLASSROOM

Mrs. Johnson has a student, Eric, in her fourth grade class. He struggles with paying attention to lectures and has difficulty completing assignments during independent tasks. Mrs. Johnson had originally decided she would just ignore Eric when he was not paying attention or when he was off task during the independent tasks. However, Eric's behavior is getting worse, he is becoming the class clown, and she is having a difficult time teaching.

She feels like she is quickly losing control of her entire class because of Eric. Mrs. Johnson is frustrated and has a positive rapport with her supervisor, so she asks her supervisor to come in and observe and to be honest with her about what might be happening in the classroom.

Her supervisor suggests that she look for opportunities to praise Eric when he is on task or paying attention during the lecture or working on independent tasks. Mrs. Johnson figures this is certainly worth a try. She is desperate. Mrs. Johnson begins her lecture and has been lecturing for about 3 minutes when she notes that Eric is paying attention. She says: "Thank you, Eric, for paying attention while I am talking. I appreciate that." Eric continues to pay attention for another 2 minutes. Because Eric is still paying attention, Mrs. Johnson asks him a question that she knows he can answer, and when he answers correctly, she says, "Eric, that answer is right on target. Thank you." When directions are given for an independent task and Eric has completed two of the questions, Mrs. Johnson approaches Eric and says, "Eric, I am really proud of you for getting those two questions right. Congratulations."

Behavior-specific praise may be implemented differently at the secondary level because some students at that level do not like to be praised in front of their peers. They may be accused of being the teacher's pet.

Mrs. Huber utilizes behavior-specific praise in her high school English class in a different way. When she gives an independent assignment for students to complete, she moves around the room and carries a pad of sticky notes with her. She takes a couple of actions. She goes up to some students and states privately, "Bill, that is an excellent answer. It is clear that you understand this assignment because you have captured the relevant points."

She continues moving around the room. When she gets to Megan, she jots down a note that says, "Megan, thank you for getting 10 of those questions answered and staying with the assignment." With some students, she finds that they like the verbal feedback, but other students like the personal note. They are seen putting it in their pocket or purse and taking the positive note with them.

WHAT THE RESEARCH SAYS

Studies for more than 50 years have shown the importance of positive reinforcement and its association with academic benefits. Teachers foster positive interactions when they increase the number of times that students are recognized and reinforced for appropriate behavior (Epstein et al., 2008).

Behavior-specific praise eliminates problem behaviors, reduces the need for reprimands, and increases positive interactions with students (Reinke, Lewis-Palmer, & Merrell, 2008; Stormont & Reinke, 2009).

Brophy (1981) determined that teacher praise is most effective for students when it is behavior specific. Early research (Anderson, Evertson, & Brophy, 1979), however, found that as little as 5 percent of praise statements were behavior specific. While any praise is a good practice for a classroom teacher to use, behavior-specific praise is more effective. Generalized praise such as "Good job" or "Way to go" is better than no praise, but statements like "Thank you for picking up that piece of paper" tell the student what you like.

Previous studies have found that a ratio of praise to correction should be four to one (Simonsen, Fairbanks, Briesch, Myers, & Sugai, 2008). Studies have also found that teacher praise increases and maintains behavior (Hall, Panyan, Rabon, & Broden, 1968).

Allday and colleagues (2012) found that, in teacher training of general education teachers who were working with students at risk of emotional and behavioral disabilities, teachers increased their use of behavior-specific praise, the students targeted in the study increased their task engagement, and the use of corrective statements decreased. This study showed that providing general education teachers with a short, 30-minute training every 3 days that incorporated self-selected goals and performance feedback was effective.

In a study conducted by Sutherland, Wehby, and Copeland (2000), it was found that behavior-specific praise increased the on-task behavior of students.

Conroy, Sutherland, Snyder, Al-Hendawi, and Vo (2009) have found that the characteristics of effective praise include the following characteristics:

1. Contingent on the desired behavior and provided immediately following the behavior

2. Behavior specific

3. Focused on effort and process

4. Teacher initiated

Fry (1983) found that reduced praise combined with high rates of reprimands led to a deteriorating cycle of inappropriate behaviors. Children with behavioral problems need more praise, not less, than other students.

Van Acker and Grant (1996) found that some teachers fail to attend to desired behaviors of students with behavior problems. What may be happening is that the teacher is so glad the student is being quiet that the teacher chooses to say nothing for fear that the student will start acting up.

A study led by Eddie Brummelman (2014) in *HealthDay News* warned against the use of exaggerated compliments for students with low self-esteem. Such exaggerated compliments may put too much pressure on students with a low self-concept. Inflated praise was defined as a compliment that included an additional adverb or adjective such as *incredibly* or *super* or *very*. The study investigated parents' use of praise on timed math tests and found that 25 percent of the praise the parents gave was inflated. The study suggests that, if you relay to a child with low self-esteem exaggerated praise, they may believe they always need to do very well and therefore will choose easier tasks so they don't disappoint. This study would also support the importance of behavior-specific praise.

BASIC DIRECTIONS TO FOLLOW WHEN UTILIZING THIS INTERVENTION

Children want to be recognized when they are engaging in appropriate behavior and in the process of recognizing the child for behavior that we like, we need to give the child specific feedback about what the child did that was desirable.

1. Make sure that your praise is specific to the student, explaining exactly what you like about what the student has done. The more specific, the better.

2. Know which type of praise each of your students likes. Younger students tend to like verbal praise provided in front of their peers. Older students tend to like praise that is private and may be given either privately verbally or in writing. However, this will depend on the student because I have worked with students who were in high school who liked to be praised in front of peers. It clearly depends on the needs of the student.

3. Praise should frequently include student names because that provides a sense of personalization (Lampi, Fenty, & Beaunae, 2005).

4. Ensure that your praise is sincere. Students know whether a teacher is just making a positive statement that is not sincere and appears to be mechanical.

5. When the need for correction occurs in an interaction with a student, you should begin with a positive statement that is related to the behavior that is being taught to the student (Cortez & Malian, 2013). The student may be acting up but is staying in the room rather than running away; therefore, the student can be provided with behavior-specific praise for staying in the classroom. This practice helps students to recognize that they are making progress and shows the student that the teacher is aware of his or her progress (Cortex & Mailan, 2013).

6. Students who have behavior problems did not develop them overnight, and you may not be able to change the behavior immediately. Therefore, it is important to reinforce successive approximations. What this means is that you set a goal for the behavior that you desire and then you reinforce the student as he or she gets closer and closer to the goal. If the goal is for the student to stay in his or her seat and work on the current assignment, then you may want to reinforce the student for at least staying in the seat. Then you can reinforce the student for starting on the assignment, then for working on the assignment for 2 to 3 minutes, and so forth, until the student reaches the desired goal.

7. Avoid the use of exaggerated praise or inflated comments. Be specific in praise rather than exaggerating the praise that you are providing.

8. At least 80 percent of the comments made to students each day should be positive statements. There should be a four to one ratio of positive to corrective statements.

9. You should work to monitor your use of praise and make sure that you are providing frequent reinforcement to students. Teacher self-monitoring of praise is critical.

10. It is advisable to vary praise so that students don't take it for granted. This is a major reason why behavior-specific praise is recommended because that will ensure that praise is varied.

11. It is critical that you teach your students how to accept praise. Some students set themselves up for reprimands and have not learned how to accept praise. Accepting compliments is a social skill that must be taught. One of the mistakes that we often make is that we provide a student with praise for something the student did, and the student immediately starts acting up. The teacher then backs off and quits praising the student because, after all, the student misbehaves when he or she is praised, and certainly the teacher doesn't want the misbehavior.

Never stop praising the student because the student is testing to make sure that the teacher will hang in there. Instead, take this as an opportunity to teach the student how to accept praise.

One of the best teachers I know uses a compliment cup within her classroom. She follows the model of how to give sincere, behavior-specific praise, she gives students multiple examples of the use of praise, and she provides multiple opportunities for practice in giving compliments. Critical also is that she teaches the students how to accept compliments by saying, "Thank you." She puts each student's name on a Popsicle stick. Each morning, the student draws a name and is responsible for giving the student whose name they draw at least two compliments during the day. The student gives compliments, the teacher reinforces the student for doing so, and the receiving student says, "Thank you." The social skills the students learn generalize to other situations, and when the students see other students not in their class or a staff member, they compliment them.

We have all known people who could not accept a compliment. If we compliment them about an article of clothing they are wearing, they might respond, "Oh, it's some old thing I had in the closet." This individual has never learned the social skill of accepting compliments.

Remember these steps in teaching the social skill of accepting compliments:

a. You should model giving compliments and receiving compliments.

b. You should provide direct instruction on how to give a compliment and how to accept a compliment.

c. You should provide multiple examples of giving compliments.

d. You should provide multiple opportunities for the practice of giving and getting compliments, such as compliment cup.

e. You should reinforce students who are giving compliments and students who accept the compliments.

12. In collecting data on behavior-specific praise, you should focus on your own use of praise, and you can do that in a number of ways:

a. You can pick a 30-minute period of time during the day, preferably a period of time when you are having difficulty with the students, and audiotape your interactions with students. At the end of the day, listen to the tape, and mark down the number of general praise statements you used, the number of behavior-specific praise statements you used, and the number of reprimands you used. Chart your results, and make a goal for yourself on what you want to improve. On another day, do the same thing, and chart your results. You may then want to wait another week and tape yourself again. Look at your data, and see whether you have increased your use of behavior-specific praise and reduced your reprimands. Periodically do this, especially if you see an increase in disruptive behavior, because it can be related to your lack of behavior-specific praise.

b. At the beginning of each day, put a number of pennies in your pocket. You may want to start with 20 pennies in one pocket. Each time you make a behavior-specific praise comment to a student, move one of the pennies to the other pocket. Your goal is to move all of your pennies to the other pocket. Each day, you will want to increase the number of pennies you put in your pocket. Keep data on the number of pennies you moved, and set a goal for how many behavior-specific praise statements you use. Another option for you is to move a penny to the other pocket when you make a behavior-specific praise statement to a student and, when you give a student a reprimand, to take a penny from the pocket that has the praise statement pennies in it and move it back to the starting pocket.

c. If you have an assistant in your class or a co-teacher, you can each keep data on the other person. One teacher or assistant has a sticky note, and each time he or she hears the colleague use a behavior-specific praise comment, he or she makes a mark on the sticky note. The other person does the same thing. At the end of the day, the colleagues look at the results and make goals for themselves about what they will work on the next day.

d. This is a fun way to collect data with the children. Each student is given a dot-to-dot sheet that is not filled out. Each time the teacher gives the student a compliment utilizing a behavior-specific praise statement, the student gets to connect a dot on the sheet. At the end of the day, the teacher and the student can review how many dots are connected. The teacher keeps the completed dot-to-dot sheets and records the number of praise statements. When the praise statements are recorded, the dot-to-dot sheet can be sent home with the child, so the parent can see how many praise statements the student received that day. The system will need to be explained to the parent in advance so that the parents understand what this means.

You can also do the same thing with a blank bingo card. Each student is given a blank bingo card, and each time the teacher gives a behavior-specific praise statement, the student gets to fill in a square of the bingo card. When the students get a complete bingo card, they get some special reward like so many minutes of free time or time to do a preferred activity.

Making the Collection of Data About
Praise Fun at the Elementary Level

Draw a line from dot number 1 to dot number 2, then from dot number 2 to dot number 3, 3 to 4, and so on. Continue to join the dots until you have connected all the numbered dots. Then color the picture!

ANSWER:

Give the student or students a dot to dot with numbers or letters of the alphabet. Each time the student is praised during the day, the student gets to connect a dot. When the student connects the dots to make a picture, he or she receives some type of recognition or free time for a special project. You will want to start with only a small number of dots to make the picture in a day and then gradually increase them. If you keep these pictures, you will have excellent data on how many praise statements that a student got during the day.

Many students love to play games and especially bingo. I have seen teachers utilize this with their entire class. Give the students a blank bingo card. Each time you give them a behavior-specific praise statement, they get to color in a square of their bingo card. When they complete the bingo card, they can earn a preferred activity or another type of recognition. Teachers who have used this report that this not only improved the behavior of their students but also increased their use of behavior-specific praise statements.

A Fun Activity at the High School Level

The teacher gets a supply of raffle tickets. Each time the teacher gives a student a behavior-specific praise statement, he or she gives the student half of the raffle ticket and puts the other half in a bag or basket. At the end of the period, the teacher draws a raffle number, and whoever has the winning ticket wins a small prize. The prize might be school supplies such as sticky notes, unusual writing pens, or a notebook. I use this at the college level as an incentive for students to come back from break on time. The prizes are small, but the students get excited that they have won something.

Working With Parents on the Use of Behavior-Specific Praise

To involve parents in the use of behavior-specific praise, explain to the parents at a conference how you are utilizing behavior-specific praise with the students. You may want to hold a special meeting with all parents on the topic because, if they understand what you are doing within the classroom, they can also work on increasing their use of behavior-specific praise at home.

If you are using home–school journals with parents, where you write notes home about how the student has done at school and the parents write back to you with their comments about how the child has done at home or their questions about what happened at school, you should model the use of behavior-specific praise in those notes. Use statements such as "I was so proud of Jason today—he completed two math assignments on his own" or "Becky helped another student who was having difficulty opening her milk carton." These are specific statements that not only model the use of behavior-specific praise, but they also tell the parents exactly what their child did that was positive.

Tips for Positive Home-School Journals

1. Thank the parent for writing in the journal the previous evening and getting the journal returned.

2. Provide behavior-specific praise to the parents about what they did to help their child the previous evening.

3. Be specific about the activities that you did during the day so the parent has information to talk about with the student.

4. Provide behavior-specific praise for what the student did well during the day.

5. If negative behaviors occur, focus on how you are working with the child to improve behavior. Rather than saying, "Your child wouldn't play a game with another student," say "We are working on playing a game with another student."

6. Reread the journal before you send it home to make sure your statements are objective and understandable.

Troubleshooting if the Intervention Is Not Working

1. The praise I am providing may not be specific enough for the student. Praise such as "Way to go" or "That's terrific" leaves the student wondering what is terrific and what the teacher actually liked about what they did.

2. The praise I am providing may not be frequent enough for students. Sometimes teachers find themselves praising certain students to the exclusion of other students.

3. I may be providing praise in situations where the student has not met the criteria to receive praise (Lampi et al., 2005).

4. I need to be careful that my praise is not perceived as insincere by the students. I need to monitor to make sure that I am not being mechanical in my use of praise and the students perceive it as not meaningful.

5. My praise may not be appropriate to the needs of the individual child. As an example, I may be praising the student in front of other students, and the student prefers praise in private.

6. I may not have taught my students the social skill of giving and receiving praise or compliments.

A Checklist to Help You Remember

✓ Do I provide behavior-specific praise that focuses on the behavior that I want?

✓ Do I know whether my students prefer praise that is public or praise that is private?

✓ Do I monitor my use of praise to ensure that I am providing sufficient praise to all the students within my classroom?

✓ Do I ensure that your praise is not exaggerated but is specific in nature?

✓ Do I establish a monitoring system to ensure that I am utilizing enough behavior-specific praise?

✓ Do I teach my students how to give and how to receive reinforcement or compliments?

✓ Do I provide behavior-specific praise to parents and work with parents to suggest ways they can provide praise statements to their students?

✓ Do I collect data on whether my use of behavior-specific praise is resulting in improved behavior of my students?

Strategy 5

Supportive Proximity Control

*Building Positive Relationships
by Moving Around the Room*

SUPPORTIVE PROXIMITY CONTROL DEFINED

I refer to *proximity control* as the teacher's desk-side manner. It is the positive way you as a teacher interact with the student. Proximity control refers to the support that you give to a student by being within close proximity.

Effective teachers give lectures and provide instructions to students, but an integral part of that verbal and visual information is moving around and being close to students to provide supportive assistance and hurdle help.

Proximity control refers to your being in close proximity to students for support but not so close that the student perceives that you are hovering over him or her. The advantage of proximity control is that you are able to monitor firsthand whether each student actually is understanding what needs to be done.

When you are close to a student, you can provide supportive assistance that a student might need, but the student does not want to ask for help in front of the entire class. It is embarrassing to ask for help, particularly for an older student who does not want to take the risk of being wrong or looking foolish among his or her peers. A simple statement from you such as "What can I do to help you?" when you are close is private and respectful to the student.

When you are close to students, you have the opportunity to assist those students who may have difficulty with auditory processing. You have given verbal directions and can now move around the room to show students what they need to do or to repeat the directions.

For students who are English learners, they may not understand what you have said, and by moving around the room, you can clarify the directions.

When you are close to the student, you are also able to render hurdle help. A student may be stuck on a particular math problem and is just sitting or has shut down. As you move closer to the student, you can see what has occurred and can make a supportive comment such as, "Looks like you got three of these right, but you are stuck on number four. How about if you move on to number five, and then I will come back in a few minutes and help you with number four." Because you are close to the student, the student sees that you recognize that he or she is stuck and feels supported knowing that you will come back and help.

Johns (2011) defines proximity as "being close but not too close, to the student." Most research has defined effective proximity as within about 3 feet of the student (Etscheldt, Stainback, & Stainback, 1984; Gunter, Shores, Jack, Rasmussen, & Flowers, 1995). Proximity is respecting the individual student's space but at the same time being close enough to provide supportive assistance.

Proximity control also provides the opportunity for you to have a shoulder-to-shoulder conversation with a student. Each party is standing or sitting side by side, which may be much less threatening, particularly for older students. You can also use shoulder to shoulder when you bend down to help a student with his or her work at his or her level. This allows you to provide support and assistance to the student while not requiring eye contact, a less threatening practice for some students. In some cultures, requiring eye contact is not appropriate, and a shoulder-to-shoulder conversation is a good solution.

Hansen (2010) commented that educators communicate how they feel about a student by adjusting their distance from the student. Individuals create spaces separating themselves from others, and the size of those invisible barriers varies according to culture, age, personality, and intimacy of the relationship. Teachers need to adjust their distance according to the students' and parents' cultural backgrounds.

Teachers also have their own boundaries that are determined by their cultures and personalities. Hansen (2010) reports that teachers increase rapport by facing students, sitting at the same level, and leaning toward students. Teachers can use proximity to build relationships and enhance classroom communication by leaving the desk behind, sitting side by side when that is appropriate, and maintaining eye contact and standing near each student each day (Hansen, 2010).

Active listening is an important tool for an effective teacher, and such listening is much easier to accomplish when the teacher is near the student. Eye contact from the teacher (depending on the student's culture) and paraphrasing the student's comments are simple ways that the teacher can demonstrate that he or she is interested in the child (Minnesota Association for Children's Mental Health, 2006).

This chapter shows how you can use proximity to provide support to students, which then results in a positive classroom climate.

LIVE ACTION FROM THE CLASSROOM

Mr. Willis teaches second grade students. He has a desk at the back of his room but rarely uses it during the day because he is always moving around the room for the purposes of seeing firsthand what each of his students is doing. Craig has moved into his classroom from another district, and Mr. Willis is concerned about the information that is contained in Craig's records from his previous teacher. His previous teacher reported that Craig was out of his seat at least 20 times per day and refused to do any of his independent work.

When Mr. Willis is giving short lectures with visuals, he is moving around the classroom, so he can determine who is and who isn't paying attention. While Mr. Willis is moving around, he is giving positive hand signals to students who are paying attention, and he is commenting verbally, "Thanks, Craig, for really listening to these key points."

When he gives follow-up independent work to students, he moves around the room making positive statements to students who are working. When he gets close to Craig and notices that Craig is having difficulty with a particular question, he says privately to Craig, "How can I help you?" If he notices that Craig has answered one or two questions correctly, he says, "Way to go. You got those two questions right. Thanks for working so hard." When he comes to Craig and notices that Craig has gotten two or three questions right but has become stuck on number four, Mr. Willis uses hurdle help. He points out what Craig has gotten correct and comments further, "Looks like you are stuck on number four, and that's OK. How about if you go on and work on numbers five and six, and then I will come back and help you with number four." Mr. Willis finds that this provides comfort to Craig. Craig moves off of number four and goes on to five and six. Mr. Willis then goes back to Craig to assist him with number four.

Mr. Willis finds that Craig is not having the problems that were reported before because he uses supportive proximity control for purposes of seeing what each student is doing, but more importantly, he uses it to be supportive of his students.

At the secondary level, Mrs. Worbel teaches high school English. In her last-period class, she has at least five students who act like class clowns and who at times become so disruptive that it is hard for her to teach. She also has about six students who struggle with independent work. She knows she has to make some changes in her approach because she is losing control. With her other classes, she is able to lecture at the front of the room, and her students are able to work on follow-up independent activities, but this is not the case with this group of students.

Mrs. Worbel decides that, during her planning period, she will observe one of the other teachers and see what that teacher is doing that is working. She observes one of her colleagues and notes that her friend moves around the room continually and has no behavior problems. She decides she will utilize this approach, and her colleague has agreed to help her.

Instead of lecturing from the front of the room, Mrs. Worbel starts moving around while she gives her lecture. During her lecture, she utilizes both visual and auditory cues. She finds that the students in the back of the room cut the clowning because they know she is watching them. Moving around the room also allows Mrs. Worbel to see whether the students are actually attending to her lecture and whether they are grasping what she is saying. She also puts a supply of sticky notes in her pocket that say, "Thanks for paying attention."

As she moves around the room and sees students who are paying attention, she puts a sticky note on their desks to recognize them.

During independent work, she also moves around the room. She carries a supply of sticky notes that say, "Thanks for working so hard." As she sees students working on their independent tasks, she gives them sticky notes. While she moves around the room, she is also providing supportive assistance to her students. When she sees a student who is struggling, she asks the student privately, "How can I help you with that?"

WHAT THE RESEARCH SAYS

Proximity control is an effective behavioral intervention tool that can prevent many behavioral problems from happening (Johns, 2011). Research has shown that moving around the room, assisting, and physically and verbally interacting with students during individualized activities increases desired behavior (Gunter et al., 1995; Gunter, Countinho, & Cade, 2002).

Research has also shown that, when working with students with significant behavior problems, student academic engagement increased during independent work when the teacher or other staff member was moving around the room. In that same research, it was found that another effect of teacher proximity was increased praise (Gunter et al., 1995).

Research has shown that proximity is an effective management strategy to keep students on task, to make smooth transitions from one task to another task, and to decrease behavioral problems at recess (Lampi et al., 2005; Lewis, Colvin, & Sugai, 2000). Several research studies have also shown that proximity control has been successful in effectively including students with emotional and behavioral problems in the general education classroom (Conroy, Asmus, Ladwig, Sellers, & Valcante, 2004; DePry & Sugai, 2002; Gunter et al., 1995). McIntosh Herman, Sanford, McGraw, and Florence (2004) reported that proximity control sends a message to the students that the teacher is in control. The teacher is able to observe situations that could be volatile and can prevent behavior problems before they start (Lampi et al., 2005). Gunter and colleagues (1995) showed that an attentive teacher who is only a few steps away can decrease the occurrences of challenging behavior, thus reducing classroom disruptions.

An early study by Fifer (1986) found that, in general education classes where the teachers remained in front of the classroom, student disruptions occurred toward the back of the room and positive interactions occurred toward the front of the room.

Etscheldt and colleagues (1984) found that a child who was identified as the most disruptive out of 40 students in the classroom was less disruptive when the teacher was within at least a 3-foot radius.

In another study, it was found that, when one student was praised for appropriate behavior from a teacher who was in close proximity, there was an increase in appropriate behavior by that student, and there was also an increase in the appropriate behavior of a student in an adjacent seat (Broden, Bruce, Mitchell, Carter, & Hall, 1970).

A very interesting study was done back in 1996 as a result of some fear that computer education would interfere with the personal contact between teacher and student (Sills-Briegel, 1996). This study examined the interaction between teachers and students in a computer lab, specifically looking at how physical proximity distances between teachers and students differ between classroom and computer lab environments. In an inner-city middle school, 113 students were studied. Sixty were observed in a computer lab, and 53 students were observed in general education classrooms. All subjects were African American, and all teachers, except one, were African American. This study found more instances of teachers working intimately (defined as within 1.5 feet) with students recorded in the computer lab than in the classroom. Teachers worked more personally with students (1.5–4 feet) in the lab condition. Interesting also was that there were more long-distance events recorded in the lab than for classes. In the computer lab, teachers either worked closely with students, or they did not interact at all with students; some teachers used the computer lab as an extra conference period and left the room. The researcher determined that the very nature and design of a computer lab requires that teachers and students interact more personally. She believed that more-trusting interpersonal relationships could be built in computer labs than in a classroom.

Development of perceptions of space are gradual. Preschool and primary-age students communicate in a personal zone that is 2 to 4 feet away. As children grow, they discover that, the more they like their friend in conversation, the closer they stand, and they utilize the preferred proximity of their cultures (Hansen, 2010).

Kendrick, Hernandez-Reif, Hudson, Jeon, and Horton (2012) conducted a study of preschoolers 2.5 to 5 years of age on the playground with the teachers who were supervising and their proximity to the students. They utilized the concept of a zone model (zone defense) as a way to supervise and facilitate children's skill development while on the playground. In this model, the teachers were given a preassigned zone on the playground and were expected to focus on the children's activities, monitor for safety, and facilitate the children's social development from that assigned area. They were trained to redirect children from negative to appropriate behavior and to help children with problem solving. They were also trained in active listening. The study found that the training to use the zone model decreased the time the adults spent interacting with other adults on the playground and increased the positive interactions with the children.

Several Dutch studies have been conducted on the topic of proximity. Brekelmans (1989) found a clear relationship between student motivation and teacher proximity in physics. Another study found a link between proximity and student regulation of emotions (van Amelsvoort, 1999). Wubbells and Brekelmans (2005) talked about the importance of the teacher being respected by students when they perceived the teacher as being with it and knowing what was going on in the classroom. Proximity is a major way that the teacher knows specifically what is going on and what struggles the students are facing. These authors (Wubbells & Brekelmans, 2005) reviewed two decades of research in teacher–student relationships in the classroom and determined that appropriate teacher–student relationships are characterized by a high degree of teacher influence and student proximity. In a later study (Mainhard, Brekelmans, & Wubbels, 2011), it was found that it is possible that increased proximity between teacher and the class increases the likelihood that the teacher will engage in supportive behavior.

BASIC DIRECTIONS TO FOLLOW WHEN UTILIZING THIS INTERVENTION

When utilizing proximity control, you are able to see what each student is doing because you are moving around the room, getting close enough to see what is happening with each student.

Students know that you will be moving around the room not as a threat to students but as a way to provide support and assistance. Students who are in the back of the room are getting as much attention as students in the front or the middle of the room. You are perceived by students as knowing what is going on with the students because you are moving around. We send a bad message to students when we sit at a desk because we are showing that we don't care enough to move around and see what students need. The teacher sitting at the desk and expecting students to come up to him or her when they have a question provides an appearance that the teacher is exerting power and control negatively.

1. Your circulation in the room should be unpredictable so that you do not move around in the same way each time. This keeps students on their best behavior because they are not sure when you are going to move toward them. You should know your students, so you can target potential problem locations (Lampi et al., 2005).

2. Always pair proximity with other effective behavior management techniques such as behavior-specific praise (Lampi et al., 2005). Mendler and Mendler (2012) recommend the use of privacy, eye contact, and proximity (PEP). Proximity allows you to both correct and reinforce privately. It is recommended that you get as close to the student as appropriate and possible, make eye contact, and provide the message quickly and directly. It is also critical that you consider the culture of the student and how close you should get. Study the cultures of your students and what you can find out about how proximity may be different in certain cultures.

3. When using supportive proximity, you will want to remember the motto—be positive, be brief, and be gone. When you want the student to do something, you need to utilize proximity and make your request briefly in a positive way. There is no need to go into a long explanation of what you want done because the student may not be able to process too much auditory information or the student may not be able to remember too much auditory information.

Once you make your request, then you should move away from the student. Students need to save face, and teachers don't need to hover over them, so once the request is made positively and briefly, move away from the student.

4. Prepare small cards that you can give students as you move around the room; such cards might say, "Thumbs up," "Thumbs down," "Thank you for staying on task," or "Please chill out" (Mendler & Mendler, 2012).

5. Pair proximity with active listening when you are tuning in on what the student is saying about an assignment that the student is trying to complete. Active listening involves listening to what the student is saying to you while not making judgments based on your thoughts. It is recognizing the student's feelings without denying them. This can be very difficult for teachers to do because they want to make judgments.

As an example, you are using proximity control and ask the student what is happening with the assignment. The student blurts out, "This is too hard, and I can't do it." You then may say, "This isn't hard. It's easy." This is upsetting to the student and may result in the student shutting down and not doing any more work because you have denied the student's feeling. This is certainly not supportive proximity control. When you are using supportive proximity control, you avoid statements such as, "Try harder," "This is easy," and "You know what you're supposed to do." These statements are contradictory to active listening.

When we tell a student to try harder, we are making an assumption that they can do better, and at that point in time, they may not be able to do better. They are working as hard as they can. Many children come into schools today facing many life stressors and have high degrees of anxiety. What they can do when they are calm is very different than what they can do when they are under stress. When students perceive that something is difficult and we comment that it is easy, we are denying the students' feelings because, at that point, the assignment is indeed difficult for them, and they want the teacher to recognize they are having trouble. It is a cry for help, and supportive proximity control provides that help.

When we say, "You know what you are supposed to do," we are making a judgment. The student may not have processed the directions, the directions you used may not have been understood by the student, or the student may not remember the directions.

In supportive proximity control, you make statements such as, "How can I help you," "Tell me what you are having trouble with," and "Let's review the directions together." These statements are encouraging and say to the student that the teacher is there to help. We want to reduce stress and anxiety in the classroom.

6. Create a way to monitor your current movements within the classroom by videotaping segments of your classroom or by using some other means (Gunter et al., 1995). Gunter and colleagues (1995) recommend that data collection formats be developed to monitor teacher movement. You can place pieces of poster board throughout the classroom and mark the poster each time you go by a particular board. At the end of the day, you can then conduct a frequency count of the number of times you were in the location. You can also have an individual monitor your movement.

I was doing a workshop, and someone pointed out to me that I was only moving to the left of the audience and was not providing proximity to the right hand side of the room. Since that time, I have monitored my own movement. I am left-handed, and sometimes I wonder whether that is why I showed a preference to that side of the room.

7. Planned proximity brings a sense of order to the classroom because students know that you move around the room and can check to make sure that furniture and materials are where they should be.

8. Reflect on what types of positive support you are providing to your students as you move around:

   a. Are you providing supportive assistance? (How can I help you with this? Looks like you have these three right.)

   b. Are you utilizing hurdle help? (Looks like you got numbers one through three correct. How about if you skip number four and move on to number five, and then I will come back and help you with number four.)

c. Are you providing behavior-specific praise as you are moving around the room?

d. Are you actively listening to the student?

9. Are you respecting the student's individual space? Just as we expect students to respect our space, it is critical that we respect their space and not use proximity to tower over the students in an effort to gain power and control.

10. Are you cognizant of the cultural expectations of the students within your class regarding proximity?

11. Are you utilizing the time that you are spending moving around the room as a time to assess whether students are understanding assignments or lectures? As you move around the room, you should continually do informal assessments of your students' progress and collect data on whether students have understood your directions, whether the work is frustrating for certain students, and whether you have given too much work or not enough.

12. Are you hovering around the student? Be cognizant that this may make the student nervous or upset. Proximity control used correctly is not used to create stress or anxiety for your students; it is designed to provide a sense of calmness and acceptance of your students.

13. To collect data on supportive proximity control, use the technique explained earlier, where you are monitoring your own behavior to see if you are moving around to all points of the room. You can also collect data on problem behaviors of students in your classroom and then monitor your proximity to those particular students.

I also like to keep data on which students in the classroom are the most actively engaged and then look at where those students are seated to make sure I am not just focusing on one part of the room.

Working With Parents on the Use of Supportive Proximity Control

To involve parents in the process, explain to the parents how you are using proximity control to provide supportive assistance to your students. Provide them with some written examples of how they can utilize supportive assistance with their children at home. You might want to make a sheet that provides the following:

Avoid These Statements	Use These Statements
Can't you follow my directions?	How can I help you with this?
You weren't listening to me.	Can you tell me what you didn't understand?
That assignment is so easy.	What part of this is giving you trouble?
How many times do I have to tell you?	Let me explain this better.

Encourage parents to help children with various hurdles when they work on homework. In math, if the student is stuck on a problem, encourage the student to go on to the next problem and offer to help him or her with the difficult problem.

Here is the mnemonic HELPER to give you cues for utilizing supportive proximity control:

H—Hurdle help—as you move around the classroom, help students over any hurdles they face.

E—Examine your own movement to be sure you are moving all over the room.

L—Listen to what each student is saying as you move around the room.

P—Positive, be brief, and be gone.

E—Engage students as you move around.

R—Reinforce the students as you move around.

Troubleshooting if the Intervention Is Not Working

1. I should avoid hovering around students. I must make sure I am not invading the student's space. Proximity must be balanced with respect for individual space.

2. Ensure that I am not using proximity to single out students or to intimidate students. If I am always moving to the back of the room to keep my eyes on certain students there, it is obvious to the rest of the class and is calling attention to the students with negative behavior.

3. If I am always in the same place, I am becoming too predictable, and other students know what I am doing. They may engage in inappropriate behavior because they know I am not watching them.

4. Am I sure that I am following my plan for movement? (Remember that I was once told that I was moving only to the left of a room—I am left-handed—and once, an observer told me that I worked to make sure I moved both left and right and front and back.)

5. I may be not considering the culture of the student. I need to know the proximity expectations of each of the cultures represented within my classroom.

A Checklist to Help You Remember

✓ Do I develop a specific plan for how I will use supportive proximity control?

✓ Do I monitor my use of proximity control through videotaping or some other method of data collection?

✓ Do I use proximity control as a way to support and monitor students, not to punish students?

✓ Do I use proximity control to establish positive relationships with my students?

✓ Do I conduct informal assessments of how students are doing when I am moving around the room?

✓ Do I use shoulder-to-shoulder or side-by-side assistance and discussion with students?

✓ Do I consider the culture of the student when I am determining proximity decisions?

✓ Do I utilize active listening, hurdle help, and supportive assistance as I am using proximity?

BASIC DIRECTIONS TO FOLLOW WHEN UTILIZING THIS INTERVENTION

We all are more motivated to learn when we are being taught something that interests us. The key for each of us is to utilize our creativity to determine how we can use interests to teach the standards that are covered at each grade level.

1. Through observations, interviews with parents, and the development of interest-based surveys, you can determine the interests of each of your students. Interest-based surveys can include the following questions based on the age and level of the student:

   a. What is your favorite book?

   b. What is your favorite game?

   c. What do you like to eat?

   d. After school, what do you like to do?

   e. What is your favorite sport?

   f. What is your favorite color?

   g. What is your favorite TV show?

   It is important that you not make the interest survey too long or difficult because then it appears as another assignment that the student may not want to do.

2. For students with significant disabilities, Cannella-Malone and colleagues (2013) recommend questions to ask to prepare a preference assessment for potential reinforcement: Can the student select an item, or if not, can eye gaze be used? Can the student choose between two items? Can the student choose among three or more items? The teacher can either put the items that are potential reinforcers in front of the student so the student can choose, or pictures of the items can be utilized.

3. After you have created the survey, you can think about all the ways that the interests of the students can be built into assignments, such as these:

   a. Can I incorporate the names of the students into assignments? Can I incorporate examples during lecture periods that include names of students within the class ensuring that, when I give those examples, I am utilizing the names of all students as much as possible?

b. Can I incorporate student interests into meeting the CCSS similar to what Mrs. Anders did in her classroom?

c. Can I design worksheets that incorporate the interests of the student?

d. Can I provide assignments that incorporate interests?

- In reading, can I incorporate the driver education manual or a cooking lesson or another topic that I know is of interest to the student?
- In reading, can I ensure that students have the opportunity to learn more about specific cultures of the students?
- In math, for measurement, can students measure objects in the classroom or at home or on the playground? Can I design math problems that incorporate interest?
- In doing all assignments, whether it is science, social studies, math, or language arts, can I translate the lesson into what is relevant in the student's culture?
- Can I build in choices that are based on the interests of my students, such as in Pick Your Post, explained in Strategy 8?

4. Continually think about how you can provide group activities that incorporate the age-appropriate preferences and interests of students. There are many celebrities who are popular with certain age groups of students, so utilize appropriate activities of those individuals in various subjects. Students can read about the activities of those individuals, write about what they have done, study where they are traveling, or do math assignments based on what they are doing.

5. Many students love to solve mysteries, so one of my favorite activities is to choose a concept or vocabulary word that I am going to be teaching that day in class and hide clues around the room about it. Students have to move around the room finding the clues and then solve the mystery. This is very interesting to many students who like to sleuth.

6. Some students like comic strips, and there are many fun things that can be done utilizing this medium. There are Web sites that allow you to develop your own comic strips to assist your students in reading and writing. If you are working on sequencing with

your students, comic strips are an excellent tool. You can also have students write their own bubble statements in place of the ones in the actual comics. You can teach prediction by using comic strips by leaving off the last segment of a comic strip and having students predict what the final segment in the comic might be.

7. Another activity that many students find very interesting is to catch the teacher in a mistake. This activity serves a dual purpose. First, it's a fun way for students to apply a skill, and the students see that the teacher makes mistakes and admits to them. As an example, when students come into an English class, the teacher has written a sentence on the whiteboard, and it has grammatical or punctuation errors. The students have to find all the mistakes. In science and social studies, the teacher can post a mistake about a concept being studied, and students have to figure out what the mistake is. Another example in math would be that a problem or several problems could be posted on the whiteboard, and the students have to figure out which one is wrong. I love to begin a class with Two Truths and a Lie. I write three statements. Two of the statements are true, and one statement is a lie. Each student has to determine which statement is a lie and defend his or her answer. This is also a great way to take roll.

8. Technology provides many opportunities for interest-based interventions. Students may like specific learning games. They may like to read better when they can do so with enlarged print. They may prefer to do their math when they can complete the problems on the computer. They may prefer to write on the computer. They may wish to report on research they have done by making a YouTube video or making a PowerPoint or a Prezi presentation. They may enjoy creating Web sites or blogging.

9. Look for alternative forms of writing for students. In teaching writing to male students, McKibben (2014) notes that boys are drawn to alternative forms of writing, and to engage them, she encourages the use of action stories that involve adventure, comics, graphic novels, and humor.

10. When utilizing reinforcement or consequences, ensure that you know the preference of the student. There is a great deal of variation in what students like to do and what students don't like to do. A common example is that some schools utilize suspension as a consequence when students misbehave when, in actuality, it may be a reinforcer for some students. Rather than come to school, some

students would love to have time to stay home and watch TV or wander around town. Teachers may send students to the office, thinking that this is a consequence when, in fact, the students love to go to the office because there are many interesting things happening there. It is where the action is. When students don't get their work done, some teachers have them stay in the classroom to eat their lunch. That is actually the preference of some students because they get more individual attention from the teacher and find the lunchroom aversive. At times, it is complex to determine what the preference of the student is versus what is not. While some students can tell us their preferences, others show them by their actions.

11. To collect data on whether this intervention is effective with the student, the teacher can chart how the student does without the use of interest-based interventions. When I was working with a secondary student who was a reluctant reader, I tested the student on his reading recognition and comprehension skills before I instituted the intervention of designing his reading program around the *TV Guide*. I was seeing progress along the way, so I continued to utilize the intervention. At the end of the year when I conducted the posttest, the student had made 2 years of progress in both reading recognition and comprehension.

You can provide the typical assignments that you provide in mathematics and record the number of problems that are completed by the student. I suggest that you chart the number of problems that are completed by the student for at least 1 week's period of time. Then provide problems that incorporate the interests of students, such as writing problems that include the students' name in the problem or focus on favorite characters or activities. You can then chart the number of problems completed for at least 2 weeks and analyze the data to determine whether more problems are completed when the interest-based interventions are utilized.

Working With Parents on the Use of Interest-Based Interventions

To involve parents in interest-based interventions, interview the parents to determine the specific interests of the child. Ask the parent questions such as the following: What does your child like to do in his or her free time? With whom does your child like to play or spend time? Does your child like to help you with any specific activities? Turnbull, Turnbull, Erwin, Soodak, and Shogren (2011) recommend these questions: "What makes your child smile and laugh? What brings out the best in your child? What is your child especially good at doing? What gets your child to try new things?" (p. 196).

Once the interests are determined and interest-based interventions are implemented, provide homework for the student that is based on the student's interests. As an example, if the child shows interest in cooking and you are working on measurement, have the student make a recipe utilizing measurement skills. Before you provide homework assignments to students, it is important to know what the resources of the parents are and what the culture of the family is, so you are aware of that when planning. As an example, students in one class were working on measurement. The teacher had planned to have the students take measurements of their bedrooms, and the teacher thought that the students would be very interested in doing such an assignment. However when reviewing the situations in which the students lived, the teacher realized that about 10 percent of her students did not have a bedroom.

Capitalize also on the interests of parents. Begin your parent conferences with topics that you know the parent is interested in. You can learn about the interests of parents by listening to what their children say they like to do. You also can learn about the interests of the parents by talking with previous teachers who have worked with them. Starting the parent conference with parent interests can establish a positive relationship with the parent and may result in the parent wanting to come back for future conferences because you have established rapport and made the parent feel comfortable.

Another Example of an Interest-Based Survey Done With a Group of Students

You can do this one with a group of students as a This or That activity:

On one side of the room, place a large sign that says, "This."

On the other side of the room, place a large sign that says, "That."

Ask the students these questions, and request that they go to the side of the room that meets their preference. (Students have the option of standing in the middle if they like both or if they don't like either one. After each response, the students can explain their answers. This is a fun activity, and it provides movement for students.)

Do you prefer—This—Carrots—or That—Apples

Do you prefer—This—Corn Curls—or That—Potato Chips

Do you prefer—This—Watch TV—or That—Play Games on a Computer

Do you prefer—This—Read a Book—or That—Play Outside

Do you prefer—This—Work Alone or That—Work With a Partner

Do you prefer—This—Science—or That—Social Studies

Do you prefer—This—Write a Story—or That—Play a Game

Troubleshooting if the Intervention Is Not Working

1. I may have failed to adequately identify the interests or preferences of the student, or I may have identified them and they have changed over a period of time. Adults change interests, and so do children.

2. I may have failed to incorporate names of my students in class in an equitable manner. I may find myself using some students' names more than others, and by doing so, I am disenfranchising the students whose names I did not use.

3. I may not have incorporated the actual interests of students in activities throughout the day.

4. I may not have incorporated a variety of the student's interests, and the student tires of what I am utilizing.

5. I may not have interviewed the parents to determine the preferences of the student.

A Checklist to Help You Remember

✓ Do I interview parents and students and observe my students to determine their interests or preferences?

✓ Do I conduct interest surveys or preference assessments to determine what interests my students currently have?

✓ Do I include the names of my students whenever possible in assignments?

✓ Do I utilize age-appropriate interests as much as possible?

✓ Do I incorporate interests of students throughout the day in various assignments?

✓ Do I build in choices that incorporate student interests?

✓ Do I make sure that the reinforcers that I am utilizing are appropriate and relevant for the student?

✓ Do I incorporate fun activities in my class to make sure that I hold my students' attention?

✓ Do I include a variety of interests in my activities?

✓ Do I provide homework assignments that incorporate interests of students?

✓ Do I collect data to see if what I am doing is improving the behavior of the students?

Strategy 7

Premack Principle

The Student First Does the non-Preferred Behavior to Do the Preferred Behavior

Grandma's Law

PREMACK PRINCIPLE DEFINED

The Premack Principle, named after David Premack in 1959, is based on the premise that the completion of a lower-probability action can be reinforced by following it with a higher-probability action (Jaspers, Skinner, Williams, & Suecker, 2007). The Premack Principle happens when a frequently occurring behavior is used to reinforce a particular behavior that is not occurring at all or seldom (Wiley & Heitzman, 2001).

The Premack Principle is often referred to as Grandma's Law. Eat your peas before you get your dessert. The completion of the lower-probability action, eating the peas, is reinforced by getting to have dessert—the higher-probability action.

Many programs for children with ASD use the first–then approach with visual cues. The student must first complete the non-preferred activity, and then the student gets to engage in the preferred activity. Always provide a visual cue to help students focus on what they must do first in order to gain the preferred activity.

LIVE ACTION FROM THE CLASSROOM

Mrs. Killebrew teaches third grade at her school. She has three children with autism in her classroom and, in working together with the special education teacher and the occupational therapist, they decide to utilize the Premack Principle.

The special education teacher uses a first–then schedule with the children where she posts a picture of what they need to do first—a non-preferred activity such as a writing or math assignment. Next to that picture, she posts what they get to do then, which is a preferred activity such as reading a book about a topic they love or getting to draw a picture.

Mrs. Killebrew agrees that she wants to do this with the children with autism when they are in her general education classroom, and that sparks her thinking that she can use the Premack Principle with her other students in some areas. Her students seem to love the math games that she has designed but are not as eager to do any math worksheets. As a result, she decides to use the Premack Principle, where the students need to work for 15 minutes on their worksheets together with the manipulatives that she provides, then they can play a math game of their choice for 10 minutes. She posts a visual for the class: First—math worksheets (she uses a picture of a math worksheet) and Then—a math game (she uses a picture of a math game).

She requires the students to proofread their worksheets to prevent them from rushing through the sheets and doing them incorrectly. She notices a marked difference between the work completion prior to the initiation of the Premack Principle and after its implementation. She is so pleased with the progress of her students that she decides to work with the parents to provide homework that incorporates the Premack Principle. She sends home one independent math assignment and also sends home a math game for each student that is appropriate to the specific math skill. She explains to the parents that the children should do the independent assignment first and then they can play the math game.

To get feedback on the homework plan, she sends the parents a brief homework evaluation sheet—did your child complete the required independent worksheets? How long did it take him or her to do the sheets? This allows her to see if this principle is making it easier for the parents to get their children to do their homework.

At the high school, Mr. Jergens utilizes the Premack Principle in his social studies class in several ways. After he lectures, Mr. Jergens provides a written assignment to reinforce what he has lectured about. If students complete the written assignment during class—the non-preferred activity—then he exempts them from doing any homework that night—the preferred activity. He has found that this has increased the amount of work that is done in class. If students have read the text prior to the lecture—the non-preferred activity—and are able to answer three questions that show that they read the material, then their written assignment is reduced—the preferred activity.

If students have an A in their class when it is time for finals, then they are exempt from having to take the final. This is a big motivator for his students.

WHAT THE RESEARCH SAYS

Banda, Matuszny, and Therrien (2009) found that the high preference (high-p) strategy was used to modify math assignments to increase student motivation.

Vostal (2011) found that, for the Premack Principle to be most effective in math, teachers must determine the tasks that result in student disengagement, assess the student's preferences in math, create math practice assignments, implement and monitor the strategy, and fade the strategy.

Houtz and Feldhusen in an early study in 1976 in math found that, with a group of fourth grade students who were expected to do math worksheets and then were reinforced with free time, the free time was not effective. They determined that free time might not be reinforcing to all students. Therefore, the key is finding what is reinforcing to the student. Free time in this group was not reinforcing enough for the students to want to do the math worksheets.

Wiley and Heitzman (2001) advocated the use of the computer as a reinforcing activity. Technology is a powerful instructional tool and is reinforcing for many students and therefore provides excellent opportunities for the Premack Principle.

At the college level in an upper division class (Messling & Dermer, 2009), students were expected to attend the lecture and to submit notes for each day's reading assignment. Then they could use their notes for a later test. This was very motivating to the students.

In two studies that dealt with getting children to eat non-preferred foods, Brown, Spencer, and Swift (2002) trained parents successfully to motivate children to consume less-preferred foods using preferred foods as the reinforcer. In another study (Seiverling, Kokitus, & Williams, 2012), when students took single bites of non-preferred foods, they were provided with a break from the meal.

A study was also found where the Premack Principle was utilized in the quality performance of service employees at a fast food restaurant chain. If the quality of their performance exceeded baseline at a targeted workstation, they gained access to work time at their favorite station. The results showed improved work performance of the employees (Welsh, Bernstein, & Luthans, 1993).

Because many teachers are working with students with attention deficit hyperactivity disorder (ADHD), this is an interesting study. Based on the Premack Principle, in a study done by Azrin, Vinas, and Ehle (2007), physical activity availability was used as a reinforcer for attentive calmness of children with ADHD. The two 13-year-old students were very disruptive and off task a great deal of the day. The boys were expected to have 15 minutes of attentive calmness, and then they received a 5-minute period of activity. The behavior of the students was notably improved as a result of this use of the Premack Principle.

BASIC DIRECTIONS TO FOLLOW WHEN UTILIZING THIS INTERVENTION

When choosing to use the Premack Principle, it is critical that you know the specific activities that are high-probability reinforcers, what is reinforcing to the student. If Grandma tells you to eat your peas before you get dessert, Grandma has made an assumption that you like the dessert. But imagine if the dessert is rhubarb pie and you hate rhubarb pie, then Grandma's idea has failed. However if Grandma says eat your peas and then you get brownies, if you love brownies, that is a high-probability reinforcer.

1. Make sure your reinforcers are actually reinforcing to the student.

2. Use reinforcer surveys or observations or parent or student interviews to determine what is reinforcing to the student.

3. Be very careful that you expect the student to complete the low-probability task, the undesired activity, for an adequate amount of time based on developmental level and a baseline that tells you how often the student is engaging in the task before the student can do the desired task. As an example, if the student is writing no sentences in his or her journal when requested, you may want to consider having the student write two or three sentences, and then the student can do the desired activity of drawing for 1 minute.

4. To determine how long you should have the student do the non-preferred activity, conduct a baseline so that you see how many math problems, as an example, the student is currently doing. If you see that consistently the student is not doing any math problems and you have determined that the student is able to complete the math problems at that specific grade level, then you will want to start slow so the student can achieve success, for instance having the student do two or three math problems before getting the preferred activity at 1 minute.

5. Make sure that the non-preferred activity that you wish the student to engage in is at the appropriate level for the student. Through achievement testing and observations, you need to determine whether the activity is at the correct level. If you are expecting the student to complete math problems at a third grade level, you need to make sure the student is actually able to complete those problems independently. Never make the assumption that the student should be able to do the work; actually assess the level the student is able to do independently.

6. Gradually increase the amount of time that the student is to engage in the non-preferred activity before getting to do the preferred activity. In the case of the math example above, from two to three math problems, you then increase the number of math problems to be completed to five before getting to draw for 1 minute. You may work up to 10 problems in order to draw for 2 minutes.

7. As much as possible, utilize visual cues in order to help the student remember what the student will get if he or she does the non-preferred activity. Always with a first–then activity, utilize picture cues.

8. To collect data, keep a record of how many assignments the student is doing without the use of Premack Principle. You will probably want to collect this data for at least a week to get a baseline on the specific behavior. Then you can incorporate the Premack Principle, where you expect the child to do one non-preferred activity before the child does the preferred activity. You may want to keep data on this for about 2 weeks to make sure the behavior is stabilized. Then you can expect the child to do two non-preferred activities before the child does the preferred activity. Again, I would recommend that you get the behavior stabilized for 2 weeks before moving on. After that period of time, you will want to review the data to see how effective the Premack Principle is.

Working With Parents on the Use of the Premack Principle

To involve the parent, determine whether the parent ever uses the Premack Principle for getting the child to eat his or her meal before getting dessert or finishing up homework before getting to play computer games. Work with the parent to determine preferred and non-preferred activities for the child. For homework assignments, consider providing one or two assignments that are worksheets and then add in a fun assignment for the student to do. The student has to do the required assignment and then gets to do the fun assignment. Work with the parent to develop first–then activities. Show the parent how to do an activity where the child has to do a task first and then gets to do the preferred task next. Always encourage the parent to provide visual cues.

Figure 7.1   Some Examples of the Premack Principle

FIRST ⟹ THEN

FIRST	THEN
Do three math problems.	Draw a picture.
Write four sentences in your journal.	Read your preferred book for 5 minutes.
Work on your science project for 15 minutes.	Choose one of three free time activities.
Clean out your desk for 10 minutes.	Talk with your neighbor for 5 minutes.

Troubleshooting if the Intervention Is Not Working

1. I may not have identified correctly the high-probability reinforcer, or the reinforcer may have been successful at one time and is no longer.

2. I may be expecting a student to do the low-probability task when the student is not able to do it because it is not within his or her independent level.

3. I may have not assessed the appropriate level at which the student is functioning.

4. I may be expecting a student to engage in the low-probability task for too long before providing the high-probability reinforcer.

5. I may be providing too much time for the high-probability reinforcer based on the amount of time the student had to engage in the low probability task.

A Checklist to Help You Remember

✓ Do I identify the high-probability reinforcer that is appropriate for the student?

✓ Do I identify the low-probability activity that I want to increase?

✓ Is the low-probability activity at an appropriate level for the student to complete independently?

✓ Do I thoroughly assess the student to learn his or her independent level and the reinforcers that work?

✓ Do I start out with a short amount of time for the low-probability activity and match that with a short amount of time for the high-probability reinforcer?

✓ Do I gradually increase the time that the student must spend on the low-probability activity before getting the high-probability reinforcer?

✓ Do I involve the parent in the planning process?

✓ Do I incorporate Premack Principle in homework?

✓ Do I collect data on whether the Premack Principle is resulting in increased achievement?

Strategy 8

Choices

Empowering Students by Giving Them Choices

CHOICES DEFINED

Choice making involves the expression of preferences and provides students with the opportunity to select between two or more choices (Green, Mays, & Jolivette, 2011). Choice in instructional assignments presents the student with two or more activities from a menu of choices developed by the teacher. The student is then able to select the activity he or she wants to complete (Harlacher, Roberts, & Merrell, 2006).

LIVE ACTION FROM THE CLASSROOM

Mr. Sandman teaches fourth grade and provides choices whenever possible within his classroom. He knows that it is important to teach students that life is all about the choices they make. He wants his students to have many opportunities to make choices, and he reinforces the students throughout the day when they make appropriate choices.

In math, when he gives students a worksheet that has 30 problems on it, he allows his students to choose any 10 problems. He also likes to let the students choose where they want to complete an assignment, at their desks or at round tables that he is fortunate enough to have in his classroom. He gives them the option of doing the problems on their laptops, where they are able to enlarge the print if needed.

When he gives an assignment to assist students with reading comprehension, he lets them summarize what they have read by drawing a picture, keeping a blog, writing a song, or writing a poem about it. He also always gives the students a choice of writing instruments when they have a written assignment; they can do the assignment with a red pen or a blue pen or a pencil that has a smell.

One day, he is in the teacher's lounge talking with the kindergarten teacher, Mr. Burris, about how he incorporates choice into his assignments. Mr. Burris says he thinks that the choice idea is a great one, but of course, he can't use it with kindergarten students because they are too young to make choices. Mr. Sandman asks Mr. Burris whether he could possibly incorporate choice by giving the little ones a choice between two options. They brainstorm, and Mr. Burris decides that he will try to build in this strategy by giving students a choice of snack from two items. The kindergarten children can decide which of two snack choices they want. Mr. Burris is finding that this is improving the students' behavior during snack, so he expands choice use into free time. When it is time for free time, each student is given two pictures with two different activities that they can choose. Each student has to give Mr. Burris the card that depicts the choice they have made.

Satisfied that this is going well, he then starts using choice for academic work. He gives the students a choice of the type of writing utensil that they want to use, again giving the students a choice between two utensils. He reports back to Mr. Sandman that he is sure glad he tried choice, and it is working well and teaching the children to be more independent.

At the high school level, Mrs. Benson teaches American history. Prior to this year, she had difficulty getting some students to complete assignments, and some students were disruptive in class. She has been reading about the importance of teaching students to become independent and about the importance of empowering her students. Mrs. Benson has always been a lively and creative teacher and likes to use music and art when she is lecturing. She now decides that she will incorporate a Pick Your Post activity (Johns, 2011) into her classroom after she lectures about a topic. After she lectures, she posts five or six assignments that students can utilize to depict what they have learned from the lecture. She posts these options for students: make a game about it, make a graphic organizer about it, write a poem about it, make a PowerPoint about it, blog about it, or write a song about it. Students then can choose how they will show their knowledge about the topic. Mrs. Benson varies how she utilizes this activity. Sometimes she has the students choose their preference, and the students work in a cooperative group. Sometimes she has the students individually do their assignments (Johns, 2011).

Mrs. Benson also uses tic-tac-toe for assignments and for tests. She gives each student a tic-tac-toe sheet that has nine possible assignments, and the students can choose to complete any three to make a tic-tac-toe. The squares include the following options: write a skit about the topic, write 10 true-and-false questions, write a poem, prepare a YouTube video, write a letter to the editor, make a game, make a graphic organizer, or write a song about a topic (Johns, 2011). She also designs her tests in this manner and gives her students a choice of a standard test or a nontraditional test, such as this tic-tac-toe approach. She has found that the learning menus she has created for her students have been very motivating.

WHAT THE RESEARCH SAYS

There is a large body of research about the use of choice. As an example, there has been research in the effectiveness of choosing the assignment sequence with students with special needs. A study found that students with intellectual and behavioral problems increased their time on task when they were allowed to make the choice of the sequence of the required tasks (Kern, Mantegna, Vorndran, Bailin, & Hilt, 2001).

The value of choice has been shown in research for both promoting appropriate behaviors and reducing challenging behaviors. Students who are provided with the opportunity to make choices are more likely to engage in appropriate activities and have positive interactions with their peers. Choice provides children with the opportunity to increase their motivation and independence and allows them to improve their communication and social skills (Green et al., 2011).

Choice making also promotes decision making. Opportunities for choice making are critical in providing experiences that guide an individual's later performance when encountering life choices (Stowitschek, Laitinen, & Prather, 1999).

Kern and State (2009) report that choice can reduce problem behavior even when students are given choices that are non-preferred activities, and even when students only get to choose the order in which they complete a non-preferred activity, there was a reduction in challenging behavior. In their studies, they also found that choice of materials to complete a task was a successful approach.

In an earlier study conducted by Kern, Bambra, and Fogt in 2002 with middle school science students, students could choose whether to study for a test using flash cards or fill in the blank worksheets. Students could also choose materials to be used during their projects. There were behavioral improvements as a result.

Structured choice or forced choice has been studied to increase academic engagement in early childhood programs. Such choice is defined as a choice between a limited number of interest centers. When the child was not playing in one of the low-preference interest centers, researchers presented the young child with a structured choice board displaying two of the child's low-preference interest centers. The researcher named the two choices and asked in which of the two centers the child wished to play. The results showed an increase in time spent in low-preference centers and a decrease in time not engaged (DiCarlo, Baumgartner, Stephens, & Pierce, 2013).

Morgan (2006) reviewed findings from 15 studies between January 1985 to August 2004 to determine that teachers who used preference assessments with choice making improved student task engagement more than just providing choice making. Studies used included participants enrolled in kindergarten through grade 12. High-preference activities when used with choice making showed the greatest results. Morgan suggested that, when teachers offer increased use of more-preferred materials or prompted a student to make a choice of activities, the process allowed students to access different types and amounts of reinforcement. The teacher who consistently provides a child with choices increases the predictability of the classroom, and the child may find this more reinforcing.

In an early study by Dunlap and colleagues (1994) conducted with two 11-year-old boys with ADHD symptoms, there was improved task engagement when choice making was utilized.

BASIC DIRECTIONS TO FOLLOW WHEN UTILIZING THIS INTERVENTION

The ability to make choices is an excellent life skill. Students must learn that life is full of choices, and they may make good choices or they may make bad choices, but they are still in control of the choices that they make. Therefore from an early age, we must provide students the opportunity to make choices. Such choice making empowers them to make decisions.

1. Remember to limit the number of choices depending on the age and level of students. With students who have not had experience with making choices or with young children, you will want to begin with two simple choices such as the selection of a writing instrument for

an assignment or the choice of two free-time activities. As students get used to making choices, you can add choices, but always be careful that you are not overwhelming students with too many choices. With the increasing use of computerized, universally designed materials, you can give the choice of assignments that are designed to accommodate the individual student.

Some teachers utilize tic-tac-toe activities where students choose any three of nine activities from fourth grade forward. High school students really seem to enjoy the tic-tac-toe method. When utilizing tic-tac-toe, you can intersperse easier tasks with more difficult tasks, and you can delineate the specific points that each task will earn for the student. When utilizing tic-tac-toe for a test, you can weight the different choices, so students know how many points they will receive for completing specific choices.

If the students are given two to three assignments to complete, you may want to allow them to choose the order in which they do the assignments.

Choices can be utilized in writing or spelling by making a bingo card, and the students choose any five words they want to work on in spelling that would make a bingo.

In writing, the teacher can give a writing prompt and then give the students a bingo card with 25 words, and the student is expected to choose five words that would make a bingo and incorporate them into the writing.

2. Choices can include where, when, with whom, and how. The possibilities are endless. Some examples of choices given by Johns (2011) include allowing students to choose the order in which they complete a series of assignments, completing the odd number or even number problems or questions, completing the assignment on their laptops or in writing, and completing a creative writing assignment by tape-recording and then transcribing it or writing it or using a laptop. Students can determine whether they will work in a cooperative group to complete a project or work independently.

3. Look closely at which subjects will lend themselves to choices within the areas you teach. If you are having times when students are exhibiting behavior problems, this is a good starting point. You may find that choice will provide students with a level of control that many students like to have, and because you are giving them that control, you may reduce behavioral problems.

4. Look closely at which subjects or times of the day in which students don't seem to be motivated. Students seem to have lost interest. Are there ways you can build choice into those areas of concern? Choice

can be motivating because students are empowered to be involved in the process.

5. It is important that you reinforce students for making a choice by providing behavior-specific praise; for example, "I understand why you chose the blue pen. That was a good choice for you to make."

6. Capitalize on the strengths and interests of the students when you provide the choices. As an example, if you have a student who loves technology, you may want to build in an assignment choice as being able to make a YouTube video. You may give the student the choice of doing a virtual lab. If you have a student who loves to read about the weather, that could be a choice in reading, writing, math, science, or social studies.

7. Make sure that you have thoroughly explained each of the choices clearly and with visual cues when possible. As an example, if you are utilizing the choice of doing an assignment with a blue pen or a red pen, students should be able to see each pen. If you are utilizing tic-tac-toe, you should clearly explain the nine possible choices that the student has.

8. To collect data on whether choice making is working, keep notes on which choices you give your students and which choice each student makes. For instance, if you give a student a choice between writing a poem about a topic or making a game, record the choice the student makes and how often the student makes that choice. This provides you with important information not only for your classroom but also for future teachers. This data should be recorded for future teachers who will have the student.

Working With Parents on the Use of Choice

To involve parents in choice, seek advice from them about how their child approaches tasks and what their child likes to do. Parents know whether their children like to work by themselves or with others; they know whether their child likes to play video games or watch TV. In homework assignments, you can build in choice again, giving the student the ability to choose between two or three options in homework, depending on the age and developmental level of the student.

You will also want to give parents a choice on how they contribute to the success of your class. Some parents will have the time to help in your classroom, while others will not, but the parents can make some other contributions, such as sending in needed materials. Choices empower children and parents as well.

Troubleshooting if the Intervention Is Not Working

1. I may be giving too many choices depending on the age or the developmental level of the student.

2. The choices that I am giving are not of interest to the student.

3. I may be giving uneven choices or not letting students know that certain choices are not worth as many possible points as others. As an example, in tic-tac-toe, I have to be very careful that I am giving choices that are of equal difficulty, or if they are not of equal difficulty, I have told students that they are not worth as many points. When I use tic-tac-toe for a test, I mark each choice with how many points each is worth. That lets students know that certain choices are worth more than others.

4. I may not have provided a clear explanation of the choices that the student has.

5. I may not be reinforcing students for making good choices. It is critical that we let students know that they have made an appropriate choice; otherwise, students will not continue to do so.

6. I may not be providing sufficient wait time for students to make a choice. Students who are not used to making choices may take longer to make a decision. Students who are given multiple choices, such as in tic-tac-toe, may need more time to study each of the choices before making a decision. Students who have delayed processing times will need longer periods of time to make their choices.

A Whole Array of Choice-Making Activities for the Classroom

You can use a blue pen or a red pen.

You can do the even-numbered problems or the odd-numbered problems.

You can pick any five.

You can work at your desk or at the round table.

You can choose which worksheet you want to do first.

You can either write down your answers or record them.

You can write your creative story utilizing handwriting or on your laptop.

A Checklist to Help You Remember

✓ Do I ensure that the number and types of choices are appropriate to the developmental level of the student?

✓ Do I provide both visual and verbal explanations of the choices?

✓ Do I include student preferences into the choices?

✓ Do I specify the choice options and make certain that the student understands each of the choices?

✓ Do I provide enough time for the student to process the choices that are being given?

✓ Have I reinforced the student for making a choice?

✓ Have I provided choice in homework assignments?

✓ Have I collected data to show which choices students make?

Strategy 9

Response Cards

Collective Checks for Understanding

RESPONSE CARDS DEFINED

Response cards are an effective alternative to hand raising. Rather than utilizing the practice where a teacher asks the students in class to answer a question, the teacher utilizes a response system that ensures that all students will provide an answer. As an example, the teacher can ask yes-or-no questions and give each student in the classroom one card that says "Yes" and one card that says "No." The teacher then asks the question of the entire group, and each student raises the appropriate card that denotes his or her answer. Students can also be given any question from the teacher and can hold up a card, paper, or whiteboard in response (Himmele & Himmele, 2011).

Response cards are the use of cards, signs, or items that are simultaneously held up by all students in the class to display their responses to questions or problems that are posed by the teacher. The response cards can either be write-on boards or cards where the students write down the answers, or they can be preprinted ones made by the teacher (Randolph, 2007).

Response cards can also be the use of electronic clickers where students click on the correct answer, the board compiles the answers, and the students can see the results of all of the students' answers without knowing who gave which answer. The teacher can also see the results and get a quick assessment of the number of correct responses.

LIVE ACTION FROM THE CLASSROOM

Mrs. Martinez teaches second grade and has noticed that, when she asks questions, the same students always raise their hands to answer, and the children who don't know the answer put their heads down in the hope that Mrs. Martinez will not call on them. Her three students who are English learners never put their hands up because they require additional processing time. She is eager to change this situation in her classroom and decides that she will use response cards. She decides that she will keep the response cards simple in the beginning, and she gives each student two colored Popsicle sticks. One is a green stick that has printed on it the word *yes*. The other is a red stick with the word *no* printed on it.

She is working on the CCSS for reading: literature—use information gained from the illustrations and words in a print or digital text to demonstrate understanding of its characters, setting, or plot. Mrs. Martinez verbalizes an observation about an illustration from the text. She models the correct answer by holding up the corresponding popsicle stick. She then provides at least three more examples. She instructs her students to keep their Popsicle sticks down and not to reveal their answers until she gives the signal: "Go." Mrs. Martinez gives wait time of at least 2 minutes before saying, "Go." Students have to raise either their yes or their no popsicle stick about the observation that Mrs. Martinez has made, specifically whether it is correct. Mrs. Martinez praises all of the students for participating and for raising their popsicle sticks. She then provides the answer without singling any student out who has raised the wrong-colored Popsicle stick. She then gives five more observations, and students have to raise their sticks with the answer. Each time, she reinforces them for participating, provides the answer, and explains the reason for the answer.

As she is doing this activity, she is informally assessing how students are doing—how many students are getting the correct answers, how many are not getting the correct answers, how long it is taking her students to respond, and the specific areas that are causing problems for her students. She is informally assessing, so she knows on which areas of instruction she needs to focus. She is also assessing her English learners to determine whether she is providing enough wait time for them to respond.

At the high school, Mrs. Schlouski teaches history and is currently working on the CCSS on key ideas and details (Common Core Standard-RH.9–10.2; National Governors Association Center for Best Practices and Council of Chief State School Officers, 2010): Determine the central ideas or information of a primary or secondary source, provide an accurate summary of how key events or ideas develop over the course of the text. With each of the chapters, she provides short lectures, uses many visuals, and ties what the students are learning to its impact on their lives today. She also ties what the students are learning to the differing cultures of the students in her class.

She provides an individual whiteboard to each of her students, stops every 7 to 8 minutes during the lecture, and asks the students to write down the central idea of what she has just talked about. She asks each student to write his or her response on the whiteboard and then to turn it over facedown, so no one can see their classmates' answers. She tells the students that they have 3 minutes to respond. When the time is up, she draws a student's name out of a fishbowl, calls it out, and asks him or her to share and defend the answer. She is finding that this method is reducing behavior problems in her class and is stimulating interest with her students.

To vary her use of response cards, some days she conducts her short lecture using visuals and gives the students a choice of three possible main ideas about what she has discussed. Using clickers, her students answer. She displays the survey, and students discuss the results. Another fun activity that she likes to do is to play a variation of the game show *Family Feud*. After students have given their answers, rather than showing the classmates answers, she asks them what the survey said and what the top two answers on the board are. Her students love this game.

WHAT THE RESEARCH SAYS

Research supports the positive correlation between active student participation and academic success. Response cards were found effective in whole-group math instruction. They increased active participation, academic achievement, and on-task behavior during whole-group math instruction (Christle & Schuster, 2003).

Research also shows us that there is a connection between student participation and increased learning and that teaching and learning are interactive processes. An effective way to improve student classroom behavior is to increase student participation and build academic achievement (Duchaine, Green, & Jolivette, 2011).

Response cards provide students with increased opportunities to respond (OTR). Increasing the rates of OTR has been shown to increase desired social behavior and academic performance (Haydon, MacSuga-Gage, Simonsen, & Hawkins, 2012). The use of response cards also allows the teacher to assess student learning because the teacher is able to move around the room, scan for the correct answers, and give feedback on incorrect responses. Teachers are also able to spend more time on student learning (Haydon, Borders, Embury, & Clark, 2009).

Researchers recommend a ratio of 70 percent unison responding to 30 percent individual responding (Haydon et al., 2010; Haydon et al., 2012).

A meta-analysis of the research on response cards was conducted by Randolph (2007), where he reviewed 18 response card studies and found that response cards significantly increased test and quiz achievement, along with class participation, and resulted in reductions in disruptive behavior. The studies reviewed did not show any significant statistic differences between the effectiveness of write-on response cards versus preprinted response cards.

Previous studies have shown that students who have more opportunities to make academic responses during instruction learn more than those students who are not provided the opportunities to respond (Heward, 2009).

George (2010) conducted research in social studies instruction in five emotional support classrooms that included students identified with emotional and behavioral disorders. In this study, students displayed higher-than-average levels of academic responding during the response card condition than with a hand-raising response condition. Students also displayed higher averages of correct academic responses during these conditions.

Blood (2010) conducted a study of a student response system with a group of nine students with emotional and behavioral disorders. The student response system was designed to increase students' opportunities to respond through the use of technology, especially a small, handheld device known as a clicker. Students could respond to multiple-choice and true-false questions that were posed by the instructor. Responses were immediately displayed on the screen in a graph showing the percentage of responders who chose each of the possible answer choices. The visual display of the responses allowed the students to receive immediate individual feedback and allowed the instructor the chance to provide clarification of the correct answer and reteach the concepts. The results showed that all nine participants responded more frequently to formal questions than they did when another response system of hand raising was used.

It has been recommended by the Council for Exceptional Children (1987) that, during instruction of new material, teachers should elicit four to six responses per minute from students, and students should be able to respond with 80 percent accuracy. During independent practice, students should make eight to 12 responses per minute with 90 percent accuracy. Effective academic instruction through increased rates of OTR is a way to increase academic achievement and improve classroom behavior. Research has shown that increased rates of OTR for students with emotional and behavioral disorders appear to have positive effects on academic and behavioral outcomes (Sutherland et al., 2003).

Schwab, Tucci, and Jolivette (2013) conducted a study that used response cards together with schema-based instruction. This type of instruction allows students to organize necessary information. As an example, this instruction provides a way to solve word problems that involves four steps on two types of word problems. They used the FOPS acronym (Jitendra et al., 1998), which includes the following: Find the problem type, Organize the information that is in the problem using a diagram, Plan to solve the problem, and Solve the problem. The teacher gave the student the FOPS acronym as a handout. The teacher presented a word problem, and students had to respond about what type of problem it was using response cards. Students were reinforced for accurate answers. If some students didn't respond correctly, the teacher gave more examples. The next step was to either have students make their diagrams or give them preprinted drawings, and students had to choose which drawing matched the word problem. In the third step, the teacher asked the student how to solve the word problem. The students either wrote the answer down or the teacher gave each student four response cards—one saying add, another saying subtract, another saying multiply, and another saying divide—and the students held up the correct process. In the last step, the students solved the problem and showed their answers. In their work, they combined an academic intervention with a behavioral intervention to increase the success of the students with whom they were working.

BASIC DIRECTIONS TO FOLLOW WHEN UTILIZING THIS INTERVENTION

Response cards are a wonderful way to promote active engagement of all students within the classroom because each student is involved in answering a question rather than the old standard practice where the teacher asks a question and the students who don't know the answer hold their heads down in the hope that the teacher won't call on them. The other students who do know the answer are called on frequently, and other students feel disenfranchised from the classroom.

1. Incorporate multiple ways of using response cards in the classroom to provide variety and interest for your students. From a simple no-tech set of two cards that each student has that say "Yes" and "No," which students hold at the appropriate time, to a clicker system that can provide students with the results of their input on a graph, response cards can be used in multiple ways. You can purchase small whiteboards for your students and request that students write their answers there. You can give students math problems, and they can write the answers on their whiteboards. If you are working on sentence punctuation, you can give each student a question mark, a period, and an

exclamation point. You read a sentence, and the students have to raise the appropriate sentence punctuation. You can allow the students to draw a picture of the key points from a discussion.

A fun activity that consists of response cards and movement is what I call This or That. The teacher reads a question such as, "In which state is Nashville? Is it in This—Tennessee—or That—Indiana?" You post a sign that says "This" on one side of the room and post "That" on the other side of the room. The students move to the appropriate side of the room and have to defend their answers.

2. You should incorporate wait time when soliciting answers through response cards. It is critical that all of us know the processing time of each of our students and provide sufficient wait time before having students give their responses. Some children have slower processing times than others do, so you need to make comments such as, "I'll give you 2 minutes to give your answer." We live in a very rushed society, and some of our students simply can't keep up, so we must make it easier for them. For some groups of students, 2 minutes may be too long, so it is critical that you determine what amount of wait time works best for your students. For other groups of students, such as English learners, you may find that a longer period than 2 minutes is needed.

3. Provide cues to the students. In the beginning of using response cards, you should explain how to use them and give a number of examples for students to follow.

4. When you are utilizing response cards, you should reinforce students for their efforts and for providing the answer.

5. You have to teach the students how to use response cards. You can show the students how to respond and in general how to hold up the correct answer at the right time.

6. Have students keep their cards hidden until you prompt them to expose the answers; this prevents students from copying responses from other students (Randolph, 2007).

7. Ensure that the procedures for handing out the response cards is efficient. Will you have the students pass out the whiteboards or the yes-and-no cards, or will you as the teacher pass out the items? Procedures will depend on the age and developmental levels of the students. For younger children, this may be an assigned job among other classroom jobs. Whiteboards and erasable markers can certainly be kept in students' desks at the elementary level.

8. Provide time for students to get used to utilizing response cards before using them extensively. Students may be used to the traditional hand-raising method of providing responses, so it is critical to gradually phase the new system in to your classroom. You may want to start with one or two activities where response cards are utilized and then gradually increase them according to the activities you have planned. Your goal is for 70 percent use of this method of responding, but you cannot move too fast with your students.

9. To collect data on the success of response cards in your class, conduct a baseline where you utilize traditional hand raising, and pick a student or the students for which you have the most concern. Record the number of responses they provide with the traditional method. Conduct the baseline for at least 1 week. Then when you start using response cards in one area of instruction, record the number of responses that those same students provide. You can then look at the number of responses and see which method is most effective for the students.

Working With Parents on the Use of Response Cards

To gain parent support and involvement for response cards, explain what you are doing at parent conferences, so parents will understand your use of this alternative to hand raising. Sometimes parents are concerned about what is happening in the classroom when they don't understand what is being done and its rationale. I remember the story of a parent I knew who had a child who went to another school. She approached me at a craft fair. She asked me what the school was doing dribbling in the classroom. She reported that her son kept talking about dribbling on certain days. I was picturing that the class was playing basketball at school when I finally realized that the school must have been using Dynamic Indicators of Basic Early Literacy Skills (DIBELS) for progress monitoring. It would have been helpful if the teacher would have told the parent what was being done.

For homework purposes, you can send items home for practice in using response cards. As an example, if you are having students write their responses on their own individual whiteboards, you could send the whiteboard home along with a series of questions that the student is to answer. The parent can ask the questions, and the student writes the answer on the whiteboard. If you are working on yes-and-no answers and using Popsicle sticks where students answer the questions, you can send the Popsicle sticks home along with a set of questions. In order to do this, you must have explained it thoroughly to the parent and provided clear directions. You can make a plastic bag for the students to take home that has the response cards and the activity to be done.

Ten Response Card Options

- Clickers.
- Online discussion boards.
- Individual student whiteboards.
- Individual student chalkboards.
- Index cards.
- Standing up if you agree and remaining seated if you disagree.
- Two different color Popsicle sticks—one is yes, the other no.
- Question marks, exclamation points, periods—read types of sentences, and students have to hold up the correct answer.
- This or That—ask students questions that have two possible answers. Put "This" or "That" on signs on both sides of the room, and students go to the correct answer. This can also be done with opinions. Are you in favor or against?
- Put five different answers on sticky notes around the room. Have students go to where they believe is the correct answer.
- Use fingers to rate one's understanding of vocabulary terms—four fingers means the student knows the word and could teach it, three fingers means the students knows the word, two fingers means the student has heard the word but does not know the meaning, and one finger means the student has never heard the word.

Troubleshooting if the Intervention Is Not Working

1. I may not have established clear rules about how to utilize response cards.

2. I may have made my system of responding too complex for the students. For instance, for young students or students who have never been exposed to response cards, I want to begin with two options for responses and then build up to more-complex written responses.

3. I may not have provided adequate wait time for students when presenting the questions that require the use of response cards.

4. I may not have provided adequate examples of the types of responses expected.

5. I may not have provided corrective feedback that is respectful when students give an incorrect response.

A Checklist to Help You Remember

✓ Do I provide each student with a response card appropriate for the specific activity?

✓ Do I explain to the student how to utilize the response cards and what each card means?

✓ Do I provide verbal cues when I want the student to utilize the response card?

✓ Do I model how to use response cards?

✓ Do I provide sufficient wait time for each student to respond?

✓ Do I praise the students who provide the correct response?

✓ Do I provide corrective feedback right away to students who provide an incorrect response?

✓ Do I provide a ratio of 70 percent unison responding to 30 percent individual responding?

✓ Do I involve parents in the process and given homework assignments that utilize the principles of response cards?

✓ Do I collect data on the use of response cards?

Strategy 10

Differential Reinforcement of Other Behavior

Reinforcing Other Appropriate Behavior Desired to Eliminate Inappropriate Behavior

DIFFERENTIAL REINFORCEMENT OF OTHER BEHAVIOR DEFINED

Differential reinforcement refers to the practice of reinforcing other appropriate behaviors of the student including those behaviors that are in contrast to an inappropriate behavior. Reinforcement is provided for those behaviors that compete with the undesirable behavior or can serve as a substitute. For instance, if the student is yelling answers out in class, the other appropriate behavior is that the student raises his or her hand and waits until he or she is called on to respond. The teacher then reinforces the student for raising his or her hand and calls on the student: "Thanks for raising your hand, Marcus. What is your answer?"

The advantage of differential reinforcement of other behavior focuses on the principles of reinforcement of other appropriate behaviors rather than punishing the student for inappropriate behavior. It has been defined as a positive reductive procedure and focuses on reinforcing the desired behavior while at the same time ignoring any undesirable behaviors (Gongola & Daddario, 2010).

Differential reinforcement of other behavior can also be referred to as the *fair pair*. The fair pair is the other appropriate behavior that we want in place of the negative inappropriate behavior. It is the replacement behavior that we desire to develop in place of the inappropriate behavior (Johns, 2011).

You may opt to ignore a student who engages in inappropriate behavior, which may be an effective behavior intervention in some cases. However, you must be very careful about ignoring inappropriate behavior because the behavior always gets worse before it gets better. The student is testing the limits to see how much he or she can get away with before you will provide attention. Aggression should never be ignored, and when determining to ignore any behavior, you must plan ahead for when the behavior escalates.

I remember an incident where I decided to ignore an inappropriate behavior of a 6-year-old girl with whom I was working. The specific behavior was out-of-seat behavior. I ignored the behavior. The little girl proceeded to run around the room, out of the classroom, and then was disruptive to other classes. I learned quickly that, if I would have used differential reinforcement of the other appropriate behavior, I probably would have had better success. Ignoring inappropriate behavior never works if you don't also reinforce the other appropriate behavior.

LIVE ACTION FROM THE CLASSROOM

At the elementary level, Mr. Wong teaches first grade and is having a good year, except he is challenged by the behavior of Jamar. Jamar talks out in class at least 10 times in a 1-hour period. Mr. Wong is bothered by this because his rule is that the students are to raise their hands and ask permission to speak. He is also concerned that Jamar's behavior is very distracting to the other students. Mr. Wong wonders what he is doing wrong. The other students are behaving. What is going on with Jamar?

He keeps a baseline of the number of talk outs to confirm the number of times that Jamar is actually engaging in the inappropriate behavior. He seeks help from the behavior management consultant in the district. She comes in to Mr. Wong's classroom, does three observations, and talks with

determined that the function of her behavior was attention and escape. In the differential reinforcement of other behavior treatment sessions, improvement in her behavior occurred when differential reinforcement of other behavior, along with noncontingent reinforcement, was utilized.

A study conducted by LeGray, Dufrene, Sterling-Turner, Olmi, and Bellone (2010) utilized differential reinforcement of other behavior and differential reinforcement of alternative behavior with young children in traditional, center-based preschool classroom settings. This study showed that differential reinforcement of other and alternative behavior were effective in reducing disruptive classroom behavior—specifically inappropriate vocalizations. Appropriate vocalizations were determined as the replacement behavior, and the students were reinforced with a tangible item when they engaged in the appropriate behavior.

In a study in 2013 (Nuernberger, Vargo, & Ringdahl, 2013), differential reinforcement of other behavior together with self-monitoring was used to reduce hair pulling, eyelash pulling, and eyebrow pulling in a 19-year-old female with ASD. When implementing a differential reinforcement of other behavior procedure, a reinforcing stimulus was delivered following a period of time during which the target behavior was not occurring. The young lady was taught to self-monitor her behavior, and the teachers gave her coupons that allowed her access to stickers or the computer. A preference assessment was conducted to determine what was reinforcing to her. The young lady showed that she could discriminate between pulling and not pulling her eyelashes, eyebrows, and hair. She was provided a digital clock that would vibrate for 5 seconds when 15 minutes elapsed. She then recorded whether she had pulled her hair during the time. If she had not pulled her hair, she received the appropriate coupons. She also earned some coupons for accurately recording her behavior even if the behavior recorded showed that she did pull her hair. The study showed that this intervention that consisted of differential reinforcement of other behavior and self-monitoring was successful in reducing the repetitive behavior. An additional positive element of this study was that it could be implemented in her general education classrooms when other students were present and instruction was occurring with other students.

BASIC DIRECTIONS TO FOLLOW WHEN UTILIZING THIS INTERVENTION

It is critical to identify the problematic behavior such as talk outs during a group lesson or a student hitting himself or herself or flapping hands when using differential reinforcement of the other appropriate behavior.

A clear description of the inappropriate behavior must be provided in order to determine what the other appropriate behavior would be.

1. Take a baseline to determine how often the inappropriate behavior is actually occurring. Describe the inappropriate behavior in measurable, objective, and observable terms; for example, Jenny hits herself in the face five times an hour, or Billy talks out in class without teacher permission 10 times during math independent work.

2. Once you have determined the inappropriate behavior, decide what a replacement behavior would be for that inappropriate behavior. Focus on the behavior that you want the student to exhibit. Instead of Jenny hitting herself in the face five times an hour, you may want Jenny to attend to the task that the group is doing while keeping her hands down. Or you may want Billy to raise his hand before he speaks.

3. Differential reinforcement of other behavior will be most effective when the student has a number of appropriate other behaviors that can be reinforced (Knoff, 2012). Before instituting this process, make sure that the student already exhibits other behaviors that are incompatible with the inappropriate behavior.

4. It is critical that, as soon as the student engages in the appropriate behavior, you must reinforce the student for that behavior. If Billy raises his hand, you need to comment to him, "Thanks for raising your hand. How can I help you?"

5. You may want to investigate which other types of reinforcement that you can provide to the student when he or she is engaging in the appropriate behavior. You may also want to use a self-monitoring system as discussed in another chapter to assist the student in monitoring his or her own behavior.

6. In collecting data about whether the procedure works for the child, define the problematic behavior in measurable, objective, and observable behaviors, and then collect data on the behavior for a week, collecting data throughout each day. Then look at the data to determine whether the behavior is occurring at a certain time of day in a certain subject or whether it is happening on one day more than the other days of the week. Then collect data on the problematic time of the day. Gongola and Daddario (2010) recommend using a golf counter or masking tape on your arm to make the

process simple. Each time the student exhibits the undesirable behavior, click the counter or make a tally mark on the masking tape. There are also a number of computerized programs that allow you to collect data.

Once you have the data, you can then determine when and how you will utilize differential reinforcement for inappropriate behavior. After you have determined the behavior and the specific time of day that the behavior is occurring, implement the plan with the recognition for the other appropriate behavior.

Working With the Parent on the Use of Differential Reinforcement of Other Behavior

To gain support from the parent in using differential reinforcement of other behavior, explain the specific behavior for which you have concern. Explain to the parent how you wish to work together to improve the child's behavior. Talk to the parent to see if they are seeing the same behavior at home. If they are seeing the same behavior at home, you can work together to plan a differential reinforcement approach. If the parent is seeing a different behavior of concern at home, offer assistance to the parent.

Figure 10.1   Steps to Take in Differential Reinforcement of Other Behavior

Define the inappropriate behavior.

Define the positive behavior that is incompatible with the inappropriate behavior.

Develop a plan to reinforce the student for the positive incompatible behavior.

Troubleshooting if the Intervention Is Not Working

1. I may not have reinforced the student quickly enough or not enough when the student engages in the appropriate behavior.

2. I may be providing more reinforcement for the inappropriate behavior than for the appropriate behavior. If the student is getting a lot more attention by talking out in class than he or she is getting from raising his or her hand, the student is not going to change the behavior. He or she may want attention and will take it however he or she can get it—negative or positive.

3. I may not have found an incompatible behavior that is appropriate as an alternative behavior.

4. I may have identified an incompatible other behavior that is not within the repertoire of the student. The student may not know how to engage in the appropriate behavior. If that is the case, I will have to teach the student the appropriate behavior.

5. I may not have clearly identified the inappropriate behavior.

A Checklist to Help You Remember

✓ Do I clearly define the inappropriate behavior that I want to change?

✓ Do I clearly define the other appropriate behavior that is in the student's repertoire?

✓ Do I determine what reinforcement is resulting from the inappropriate behavior so that I can determine a meaningful reinforcer for the student when the student engages in the other appropriate behavior?

✓ Do I immediately reinforce the student for engaging in the other appropriate behavior?

Strategy 11

Fading

*Providing Maximum Cues and
Slowly Removing the Cues to
Ensure Errorless Learning*

FADING AS AN ERRORLESS LEARNING TOOL DEFINED

Errorless learning is a specific strategy designed to reduce incorrect answering, so the student gains mastery over lesson content. In errorless learning, the teacher embeds the correct answer or enough information within the question so that the student has a strong probability of responding correctly.

Fading can be defined as the process of providing maximum cues to a student when teaching a task and then slowly removing the prompts or cues that are given. An important component of errorless learning is prompt fading, where the teacher gives the correct answer at the beginning and then begins to slowly fade the prompts that are given to the student.

LIVE ACTION FROM THE CLASSROOM

At the elementary level, Mrs. Krell teaches second grade and utilizes fading in several ways. In mathematics, she is working on simple word problems. She provides a word problem and then completes the problem for the students, showing all the steps she took to solve the problem. She then has each student complete that same problem together with her. She praises them for their efforts. She then has the students work together with a partner on the problem. She then asks each student to complete that problem independently.

During the next step in the process, she completes all of the problem steps for the original problem, except for one step, and the students figure out that step. During the next step in the process, she completes all but two steps of the process, and the students complete those two steps. She continues this process until the students are able to complete all of the steps of the story problem without her assistance. Step by step, she systematically fades her assistance.

Currently she has a student, Andy. Andy has autism, and he is very strong visually but has great difficulty in auditory skills. He has not been able to learn to read using a phonetic approach. It has been tried multiple times during first grade and at the beginning of second grade. Mrs. Krell has worked together with the special education teacher, Mrs. Johnson, to develop a visual approach to teach reading recognition skills to Andy. They are working first on recognition of those words that could have associated pictures—boy, girl, fruit names, animal names, places, and so on. They have developed a set of cards for each word. For instance, when working on the word *boy*, they have made a sequence of cards that show a picture of a boy. The boy is colored with a specific color, and underneath the picture is the word with the same color. They begin with the first card, which shows the picture of the boy in blue and the word in blue. The teacher then tells Andy that this is the word *boy*, pointing to the word. She then asks Andy what the word is, and Andy responds, "Boy." She praises him and does this for several trials. She then presents the next card of the picture of the boy, and only the outline of the boy is in blue and the word is in blue. She tells Andy what the word is and then asks him what the word is until he is able to respond without a cue from her. The next card, which she presents at another seating, has the picture of the boy with no color, but the word is still in blue. She gives him the prompt and then asks what the word is. The next card has the picture of the boy not in color and with dotted lines, and the word is still in color. She prompts and then asks the student what the word is. The next card has no picture but only the word appears in blue. She follows the same procedure. The next card then has all but the letter *y* in blue, the next card has only the *b* in blue, and finally, the last card just has the word. Mrs. Krell uses this for many words that have pictures that can depict them. For words that don't have pictures, she still uses color cues and provides the word first to the student, and then the student names the word. She then fades out the prompts.

were then faded were effective for students with autism who were being taught play skills. Because many children with autism show a preference for visual stimuli, teachers utilize these visual cues when teaching new skills, in schedules, and in making transitions. They recommend the use of color coding, labeling, highlighting, visual mini-schedules, and providing a visual model of what the expectations are. The advantages of providing many visual cues are that those cues can be systematically faded as the students learn the skills.

Murphy, Figueroa, Martin, Yu, and Figueroa (2008) conducted a study with students with developmental disabilities where staff members were using computer technology to teach visual–visual nonidentity matching such as matching the printed word *dog* to a picture of a dog or matching a sock to a shoe. They used technology to fade clues for students. By using computer-generated materials for within-stimulus fading, they were able to teach these tasks.

Research was conducted teaching fifth grade students who were struggling in reading to use a verbalization strategy for reading. Children with reading skill deficits received specific instruction on how to locate main ideas. The children were taught and actually verbalized a strategy and then faded the verbalizations to inner speech. Students first utilized overt verbalizations; they then were taught to whisper the vocalization and then to subvocalize. Children who received the strategy instruction with feedback together with the fading procedure were found to make the most significant gains (Schunk & Rice, 1993). This study showed that we can utilize visual cues and then fade those cues, and we can and should utilize auditory cues and then fade those cues.

In another study conducted with seventh graders (McNeill, Lizotte, Krajcik, & Marx, 2006) in the area of writing scientific explanations in an 8-week project-based chemistry unit, it was found that fading written scaffolds was most successful in teaching students to write explanations when they were not provided with support. This group study specifically investigated whether you could fade written supports when there is no individualization. The question was whether the fading of the written supports on writing scientific explanations resulted in increased student learning compared to students who received continuous written supports. It was found that the fading of the scaffolds significantly impacted students' reasoning scores on testing. When they made the learning task more difficult in the short term by fading scaffolds, they encouraged better student understanding.

For students to be independent in leisure activities, the use of visual activity schedules has been found effective. Those activity schedules involve the presentation of a series of photographic or written prompts that correspond to the specific tasks in a chain of activities (Carlile, Kelly, Reeve, Reeve, & DeBar, 2013). Activity schedules have been presented visually through the use of video modeling, video-enhanced schedules, PowerPoint, and most recently utilizing an iPod touch where the individualized picture activity schedule was embedded into the device. The iPod touch for the visual schedule resulted in better attending for the students. Participants in the study completed correctly a high percentage of activity schedule components and exhibited a high percentage of on-task behaviors (Carlile et al., 2013).

BASIC DIRECTIONS TO FOLLOW WHEN UTILIZING THIS INTERVENTION

The use of fading is a very powerful process. It allows students to be successful by providing them with maximum cues and then fading those cues. It is what we call an errorless learning procedure. Students are not making mistakes; they are succeeding because of the systematic use of prompts and then the slow removal of those prompts.

1. When determining how to use the fading approach, you must assess where the student is currently functioning in a particular area and how best to teach the student using the fading approach.

2. At the beginning, imbed the correct response, which is a prompt in the question, so that the student will be likely to give the correct response. For instance, the teacher provides a question and then gives the answer, so the student can model the correct answer. If the child is expected to read a sentence, the teacher reads the sentence to the student. The teacher can have the student read the sentence with him or her, and then the teacher can have the student read the sentence. If the student has a memory problem, the teacher may want to read all but a couple of words in the sentence and have the student then read the sentence. Assessment is important to determine how gradual the fading process must be.

3. If you are utilizing a fading procedure when asking students a question, you should first read the question and then provide the answer. Then you should ask the student to answer the question. When a student is consistently responding correctly, you can provide two or more possible answers and require the student to select one (Haydon et al., 2009).

4. Many teachers use an I do, we do, you do procedure when intro-ducing students to new concepts. I believe that I do, we do, you do together, and then you do is needed to provide students enough practice and enough cues to be able to do the task. This procedure is a form of fading because the teacher begins by giving the student maximum cues when the teacher does the task and then reduces the numbers of cues in the we-do procedure. Even fewer cues are used in the you-do-together step, and as a result, when the student gets to the you-do steps, the cues have been faded gradually, and the student is more likely to be able to com-plete the work successfully.

5. You must be cautious when you start a fading procedure. You do not want to fade cues away too quickly because the student may not have mastered the skill even with the prompts.

6. You should continue to fade prompts until the student is able to provide the correct answer with no additional prompts. Continue then to move forward to more difficult problems.

7. You should use maximum visual cues when teaching because then the visual cues can be faded. With technology, it is very easy to find pictures that depict what you are trying to teach, and then those picture cues can be faded.

Using visual cues in instruction involves graphic cues, pictures, or images in combination with print, and these show the sequence of expected behavior or task completion to the students. When visual cues are utilized, the educator must decide when those should be faded (McCoy, Mathur, & Czoka, 2010).

8. Student cue cards are important supports for students to have because information may then be faded from them. These should be wallet-sized cards on which directions or instructions or mnemonics are written down for the student, and the stu-dents can carry them in their pockets. As an example, many of us learned the names of the Great Lakes with the mnemonic, HOMES. The teacher can provide a cue card for the student that says H—Huron, O—Ontario, M—Michigan, E—Erie, and S—Superior. In a fading approach, the first cue card that the student is provided will name all the lakes. The teacher can then provide a cue card that provides only the mnemonic HOMES. This is a fading approach. Another way to use fading with this

cue card is to allow the student to use it at certain times and then gradually fade when it can be utilized.

9. Fading can also be utilized when you point to an item in the room such as the clock or the picture schedule as you state, "It is time to go to lunch." These are referred to as subtle prompts (Minnesota Association for Children's Mental Health, 2006). Gradually you fade the pointing away, so the student knows what time it is just based on your verbal cue.

10. You should utilize auditory verbalizations and teach the child how to move from overt vocalizations to whispered vocalizations to subvocalizations.

11. You may be utilizing tangible reinforcers with students and are concerned that students will become dependent on those reinforcers. The use of fading will prevent that. When giving students food as a reinforcer or tickets for drawings, you should always pair the tangible reinforcer with a positive statement that accompanies it so that the tangible reinforcer can be faded away. How do you do this?

Let's look at this example. The teacher has her students on a ticket system. Throughout the day, she gives the students a ticket when they are following the classroom rules. As she moves around the room giving the tickets, she also uses behavior-specific praise to reinforce the students for the desirable behavior. The tickets given to the students are put in a basket for a drawing at the end of the day. Using the fading approach, the teacher gradually reduces the number of tickets she gives out each day while still maintaining her use of behavior-specific praise. Her goal is to eventually eliminate the use of the tickets so that the students are responding to praise only.

12. To collect data on the use of fading, choose the set of five words you wish to work on, if you are working on reading recognition. You want to start slow. Ask the student to read any he or she knows. Stress that it is not a test and you are only trying to see what words you can help the student learn to read. Then record the number of words the student is able to read. Institute the fading process for reading right after, and record the five words that the student is able to read after the fading process is over. You can collect data any time you are using fading in any subject. Think about how you can utilize fading in any subject you are teaching, and then collect data on how it is working.

Working With Parents on the Use of Fading

When working with families, explain to them the principles of fading and how you are working to set their child up for success. If you are using fading to work on reading recognition, actually demonstrate to the parent how fading works in this process. Encourage parents when they are working on reading with their children to always read a sentence first and then have the child read the sentence following the parent. This procedure prevents students from reading words incorrectly.

Encourage the parents to give visual cues to children and then to slowly reduce those cues. If the parent has rules at home, encourage the parent to post the family rules and to provide a picture that accompanies the rule. Encourage parents to take pictures to depict what they are working with the student on. Depending on the level of the student in math, give the parent examples of manipulatives they can use.

Many teachers prepare bags of manipulatives that their students can take home for homework.

Troubleshooting if the Intervention Is Not Working

1. I may have failed to utilize enough teacher prompts in the beginning of the process. I have to remember that I must always model the correct answer first. For instance, rather than having a student read a sentence to me and reading it wrong, I should read the sentence first and then have the student read perhaps one or two words from the sentence.

2. I may have failed to adequately assess the level of the student.

3. I may have faded the cues too quickly before the student has mastered the task.

4. I may not have utilized enough visual cues. Remember that visual cues are very helpful when students are beginning to do math or reading or spelling. A common criticism that we hear in the teaching of math is that we pull manipulatives away from students too quickly.

A Checklist to Help You Remember

✓ Do I assess the child thoroughly before I begin a fading procedure?

✓ Do I develop a thorough plan on how I will utilize a fading procedure?

✓ Do I outline how many trials I should use in each step along the way before I move to the next step?

✓ Do I fade tangible reinforcers at the appropriate time?

✓ Do I utilize enough visual cues and manipulatives for the student?

✓ Do I explain the process to the parents and educate them about how they can utilize a fading procedure at home?

✓ Do I collect data to determine whether the fading procedure is working with the student?

An Example of a Fading Approach to the Content of This Chapter

(If students were expected to take notes about this chapter, the teacher could give this first handout and then the following sequence.)

Note Outline #1
Three key points from this chapter include the following:

1. Fading allows students to be successful by providing them with maximum cues and then slowly removing those cues.

2. Fading sets students up for success and is an errorless learning procedure.

3. Student cue cards are supports for students that can be faded as the student masters the material.

Note Outline #2
Three key points from this chapter include the following:

1. _____allows students to be successful by providing them with _____cues and then slowly removing those_____.

2. _____sets students up for success and is an _____learning procedure.

3. Student _____ cards are supports for students that can be faded as the student masters the _____.

Note Outline #3
Three key points from this chapter include the following:

1. _____ allows_____to be _____by _____ them with _____ and then _____ _____ those _____.

2. _____sets _____ up for _____ and is an _____learning _____.

3. _____ _____ cards are_____ for students that can be _____as the student _____ the _____.

Note Outline #4
Three key points from this chapter include the following:

1.

2.

3.

Strategy 12

Function-Based Strategies

*Understanding the Reason the
Student Is Misbehaving to Plan
an Appropriate Intervention*

FUNCTION-BASED INTERVENTIONS DEFINED

Function-based interventions are those that are based on a process that
identifies the function or purpose the problem behavior serves for the
individual (Park, 2007). Behavior serves an unmet need, and function-
based interventions look at the need the behavior fulfills. Positive interventions then replace the need to engage in inappropriate behavior.

Function-based interventions were designed to address potential environmental factors that produce, strengthen, and maintain challenging
behaviors (Singh et al., 2009). Functional assessment identifies the antecedents that precipitate a specific behavior and the consequences that occur
after the behavior that may be maintaining the behavior.

Function-based interventions are those that are based on the outcomes of
the functional behavior assessment (FBA). Just like when a student is having
an academic problem, it is critical to assess the level of the child and the needs
of the student and then determine an appropriate academic intervention;
such is also the case when students are engaging in a specific behavior.

Hershfeldt, Rosenberg, and Bradshaw (2010) advocate that teachers apply function-based thinking (FBT) to problems they are having in their classroom. It is a way of thinking and a systematic process for defining behaviors that are problematic and choosing interventions that match the function of the behavior. It does not require the depth of assessment that FBA requires. It can be used as an early intervention strategy for students with mild or moderate behavioral problems.

Such thinking requires teachers to describe the problem behavior and to gather information or data about the behavior. It encourages teachers to use existing data and new data if needed. It then asks the teacher to hypothesize why the student may be behaving the way he or she is—is it attention seeking, is it escape and avoidance, or is it a sensory need that the student has. Once the teacher determines what the function of the behavior is, then the teacher can develop a plan to meet the student's need. The teacher is able to develop a replacement behavior that meets the needs of the student. FBT is a preliminary and important step prior to FBA (Hershfeldt et al., 2010).

LIVE ACTION FROM THE CLASSROOM

Mrs. Tennyson is very frustrated with one of her students, Nancy, a third grader, and can't figure out what she should do. Every morning during individual work time, Nancy throws a tantrum, where she screams and knocks all the items off her desk. Mrs. Tennyson believes in FBT and knows that Nancy's behavior is related to an unmet need. She wonders what the function of Nancy's behavior might be. She is not sure but thinks it is related to escape from paper-and-pencil tasks.

She decides that she is going to video Nancy and her personal interactions with Nancy to see what is actually happening. She invites her colleagues to come in after school to view the video and help her see why Nancy is engaging in the disruptive behavior.

After school, several of her colleagues, eager to help Mrs. Tennyson, come into the classroom to view the video. Here is what they all see. Each day, Nancy comes into class and is greeted by Mrs. Tennyson. Nancy goes to her desk, sits down, takes out her journal, and starts writing. Mrs. Tennyson is busy reporting lunch count, helping other students put their items away, and doing other necessary chores. She does not pay attention to Nancy.

Mrs. Tennyson then directs the students to turn in their journals and then to take out two worksheets from the previous day. Nancy puts her journal away and takes out the worksheets. She begins working on one of them, and Mrs. Tennyson is busy helping other students. Nancy decides to throw her pencil on the floor and rips up the second piece of paper. Mrs. Tennyson then goes over to Nancy and reprimands her.

After viewing the video, Mrs. Tennyson turns it off. She apologizes to everyone who came to help her because, after she watches the video, she sees exactly what the problem is. Nancy has been working and staying on task, and Mrs. Tennyson ignores her. As soon as Nancy starts acting up, Mrs. Tennyson goes to her and gives her attention, even though it is a reprimand. The function of Nancy's behavior was not escape from the task; instead, it was access to attention. The antecedent of the behavior was the work that Nancy was given, the behavior Nancy exhibited was throwing her pencil on the floor and tearing up the paper, and the consequence was that Mrs. Tennyson went to Nancy and provided her attention.

Now that Mrs. Tennyson knows that Nancy wants her attention, she works out a behavior intervention plan where Nancy is provided individual attention by her when she comes in and writes in her journal. When Nancy finishes her journal, Mrs. Tennyson then gives her more positive attention. As she is completing the first assignment, Mrs. Tennyson goes over to Nancy and provides supportive assistance.

Based on the function of Nancy's behavior, Mrs. Tennyson developed a positive behavior intervention plan that eliminated the negative behavior and met the function of Nancy's need.

Let's look at what is happening in Mr. Cohen's high school English literature class. Mr. Cohen has always had a policy that he requires students to read the literature selection aloud in class. He has students take turns reading a passage aloud while the other students listen. This year, Barton is in his class, and Mr. Cohen has decided that Barton is definitely the class clown. Barton spends the majority of class time making jokes and getting other students to laugh at him. He clowns so much that Mr. Cohen is unable to continue teaching and sends Barton to the principal's office.

After 5 days of this behavior, Mr. Cohen sees that this strategy of sending Barton to the office is not working. It appears that Barton likes going to the principal's office. Using his knowledge of function-based interventions, Mr. Cohen sits down to think about what is happening and decides he will review Barton's records to see whether that information will shed some light about why Barton is behaving the way he is.

When he reads the records, he discovers that Barton's reading recognition skills are at a third grade level. Barton has compensated for the fact he cannot recognize words by listening to other students read, and he is able to comprehend material well based on his auditory skills. The lightbulb goes on with Mr. Cohen. He hypothesizes that Barton is acting like the class clown in order to escape reading aloud in front of his peers. The antecedent of Barton's disruptive behavior is the expectation that he read aloud in front of peers, the behavior is that Barton clowns and tells jokes to other students, and the consequence is that Barton is sent by Mr. Cohen to the office.

Now that Mr. Cohen understands this behavioral sequence, he gets to work developing a behavior intervention plan for Barton. He announces to the class that reading aloud will be voluntary, and students have the choice about whether they wish to read aloud. He will ask for volunteers to read the literature selection and will not require anyone to read the selection. He has also decided that he will read part of the literature selection and will bring in tapes of the reading as well.

He observes Barton to see whether the pressure to read in front of his peers resulted in the class clowning. He notices now that Barton feels more relaxed in class and is attentive when a peer or Mr. Cohen is reading the selection. Barton no longer has the need to escape the class.

WHAT THE RESEARCH SAYS

When function-based interventions are utilized, there is a more distinct identification between what drives the behavior and an understanding of how to meet the unmet needs of the student.

FBA and positive behavioral supports have a strong research base in education (Horner, Sugai, & Anderson, 2010). Matson and colleagues (2011) researched three basic groups of interventions that have been identified when the function of a behavior is determined. Operant methods include reinforcement for positive behaviors (if the function is for attention) and extinction or pairing reinforcement with extinction; skill building (when the behavior is a result of escape), such as curriculum changes, communication training, self-monitoring, and social skills training; and sensory interventions (when the function is sensory) such as earphones, for the reduction of visual, auditory, or tactile stimulation.

Whitford, Liaupsin, Umbreit, and Ferro (2013) conducted a study to assess the effectiveness at the high school level of a function-based intervention across multiple settings with multiple teachers for a high school student with challenging behaviors and ADHD. Data was collected on the student's behavior, and an FBA was completed based on observations and interviews. The student spent the majority of his day in a general education classroom and received special education resource services. The student had eight classes with seven different teachers. He was described as disruptive in class. The FBA determined the antecedents of the behavior, the consequences that were maintaining the behavior, and the function of the behavior. The FBA also identified the student's preferences for activities. Target behavior was defined as off-task behavior that was exhibited by putting his head down on his desk, talking to peers, and playing with objects. The desired behavior was on-task behavior that included having all materials and actively engaging in class discussions and note taking. The common antecedent was the teacher providing instruction. The student would then talk in class about other things not related to the directions. The function of this behavior was determined to be attention but also was escape from the activity for which the teacher was giving the direction. Based on this information, a function-based intervention was developed that included all teachers giving the student a checklist that was a reminder of what was expected. The teachers also agreed to walk among the students (proximity control) to ensure that the student was remaining on task. He was provided teacher attention for on-task behavior. When he was on task for 5 minutes, he was praised. At the end of class if he had completed all of his work, he was allowed quiet time to socialize with his peers. When off task, he was also given a redirection once. Even though the research was done with only one student, it was felt to have had a positive impact on the student's behavior when a function-based intervention was utilized.

A function-based approach identifies the environmental factors that are impacting behavior (Cheney, Cumming, & Slemrod, 2013). FBA is the most effective when it is implemented when the students first begin to show ongoing patterns of minor problem behavior (Park, 2007).

Barbetta, Norona, and Bicard (2005) encourage educators to adopt a function-based approach to misbehavior. When students are misbehaving, the questions to ask are what the function of the behavior was and what did the student gain from the misbehavior. All behaviors serve a purpose, and educators have to figure out that purpose.

The primary source of the intervention in function-based interventions is the function or hypothesis about the function of the behavior (Iovanonne, Anderson, & Scott, 2013). FBA is not used to make evaluative statements about the student or to classify an individual; rather, it is a systematic process for understanding why behaviors are occurring in order to plan an effective behavior intervention (Iovanonne et al., 2013).

BASIC DIRECTIONS TO FOLLOW WHEN UTILIZING THIS INTERVENTION

FBA provides us with the necessary insight for understanding behavior. Once we know the purpose that a specific inappropriate behavior serves, we can then plan a positive behavior intervention for appropriate behavior that meets the needs of the student.

1. As you think of a problematic behavior a student is engaging in, think about the ABCs of behavior—what are the antecedents of the behavior (what happens before the behavior occurs), describe the behavior in operational terms, and then think about what happens when the behavior occurs (consequences). Analyze the sequence of events and then determine what function the behavior serves.

2. Utilize interviews and observations of the environmental events that are triggering behaviors (Wells & Axe, 2013).

3. As you think about the problematic behavior, try to determine what the function of the behavior is—access to attention or power and control, escape and avoidance, or sensory issues. Once you have determined what the function of the behavior is, think of a way that you can meet that student's need when the student is engaging in appropriate behavior. It is possible that the behavior may have more than one function. As an example, Jessica could be throwing tantrums to get attention and because she is bothered by the high threshold of noise within the room.

4. As you reflect on inappropriate behavior, make sure that the behavior is not related to cultural differences. For example, the student may refuse to give you eye contact because, in his or her culture, that is a sign of disrespect.

5. It is critical that you base your positive behavior interventions on the information you have gained from the FBA information. At times, teachers and other personnel spend a great deal of time determining the ABCs of behavior and the purpose of the behavior but then do not plan positive interventions based on the information they have gathered. Some people are looking for set interventions that work with every student, and this is ineffective. One size clearly does not fit all when investigating appropriate behavioral interventions. Unless you individualize your interventions, you cannot establish an effective system.

6. In keeping data, I like to keep a log of the ABCs of behavior. When the student engages in an inappropriate behavior, log what the antecedent was and what the consequence of the behavior is. By keeping a log and reviewing it often, you will begin to see patterns of behavior—the child puts his head down on the desk and refuses

to do his work when the teacher gives the child a math worksheet, and then the teacher has the student go to the office.

Once you begin to see this pattern, you know that you need to see what problems the student faces when doing the assignment. You may also see that the student escapes doing math by putting his head on his desk. By tracking this behavior, you can utilize FBT to come up with appropriate alternatives.

Figure 12.1   The Process of Functional Assessment

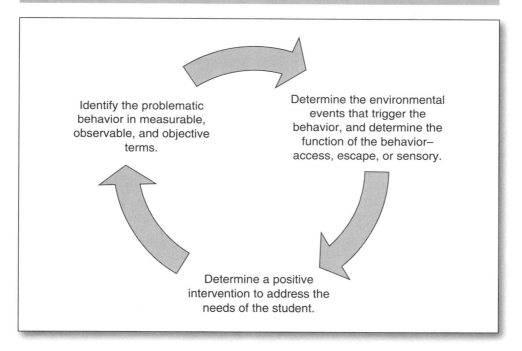

Identify the problematic behavior in measurable, observable, and objective terms.

Determine the environmental events that trigger the behavior, and determine the function of the behavior–access, escape, or sensory.

Determine a positive intervention to address the needs of the student.

Working With Parents to Determine Functions of Target Behaviors

When working with parents, ask them about the behaviors of concern for the student. Seek input from the family about possible functions of the behavior. Ask the parents if they are able to identify triggers that seem to upset the student:

1. Are there specific activities that the student does not like to do?

2. Does the student require a great deal of attention?

(Continued)

(Continued)

3. Does noise or being in a crowd upset the student?

4. Does the student show anxiety in some situations?

5. Does the student become upset when his or her routine or structure is changed?

Once you have been able to determine the function of the student's behavior, share the information with the parent, and discuss how you are going to positively meet the needs of the student.

What You Can Do When You Discover the Possible Function of Behavior

If the Function Is:	Consider This:
Access to attention or power and control	Am I giving the student positive attention for appropriate behavior, or am I giving the student attention for negative behavior? Am I giving the student enough opportunities for power and control, such as providing choices? Am I reinforcing the student when the student is assisting other students?
Escape and avoidance	Is the activity I am giving the student developmentally appropriate? Am I giving the student too much work to do at one time? Are there other ways I could present the material? I am expecting the student to learn?
Sensory	Are there specific environmental factors that are bothering the student—too much noise, fluorescent lighting, clutter, too many people? Is the student under-stimulated by the environment? Is the student overstimulated by the environment? Does the student have adequate opportunities for movement?

Troubleshooting if the Intervention Is Not Working

1. I may determine the function that I hypothesized for the student's behavior is the incorrect one. At times, behavior appears to meet a function but does not. It is also possible that the function of the behavior may be multiple in nature. For instance, a student may yell and scream when walking into a particular room, and we determine that the function of the behavior is escape when in fact the student may not want to go in that room because of the fluorescent lighting or the high level of

noise. If we reduce noise or cover the lighting, the student may not want to escape the environment.

2. If the function-based intervention is not working, ask another colleague to observe the student. A team approach often works best. Sometimes when we are working with a student, we get too close to a situation and can't see what is really going on with the student. Collaboration is key when conducting FBA. A good observer is someone who can both look at the behavior as well as the curriculum and instruction of the student. It may be that the curriculum and instruction is inappropriate for the student.

3. I may be the trigger for the inappropriate behavior. What can I do to change the antecedents of the behavior? When we are looking at the antecedents of the specific behavior, I must first look at my own behavior to determine what I am doing that could be impacting the behavior. This is extremely difficult for all of us to admit, that we may be the source, but we must monitor our own behavior to see if we are the problem. Perhaps our voice tone or the words we are using are bothersome to the student.

I remember hearing an interview with Temple Grandin, a very successful individual with autism. She commented that certain vocabulary words conjured up negative memories for her, and she would become very upset when someone used one of those words.

At another time, I was observing in a school, and the teacher was reading a story about a mother. Suddenly the 8-year-old stood up, started screaming, and ran out of the room. The teacher could not figure out what had happened. It turned out that the child's mother had been arrested the night before, and the child had been taken into foster care.

4. I may not have kept a log of the behavior and therefore am not seeing patterns of behavior.

A Checklist to Help You Remember

✓ Do I act like a detective in analyzing the behavior?

✓ Do I explore my own behavior to determine whether I am engaging in a behavior that may be causing the student to behave in the way he or she is behaving?

✓ Do I collect data on the behavior?

✓ Do I investigate the ABCs of the behavior and utilize that information to plan appropriate, positive interventions?

✓ Do I investigate the possible functions of the behavior and determine what I can do to meet the student's unmet need?

✓ Do I work together with the parent to plan function-based interventions?

Strategy 13

Strength-Based Strategies

Capitalizing on the Strengths of Your Students

STRENGTH-BASED INTERVENTIONS DEFINED

Strength-based interventions are those that utilize the strengths of the student to engage him or her in meeting the requirements within the environment. In strength-based interventions, we focus on what the child does well and what characteristics of the student are positive in nature. We then build on those strengths.

As an example, you note that the student is very helpful to others. You may want to utilize that strength to have the student engage in peer tutoring. The student is an excellent creative writer but does not like mathematics. You can look for ways to build writing into math skills.

In some cases, what sometimes is characterized as a weakness can actually be seen as a strength for a student. As an example, a student with ADHD may be very active and has a high degree of energy. Such a high level of activity may be viewed negatively, but in a strength-based approach, the activity could be viewed as a strength because many activities require a high degree of energy.

Michael Phelps, the Olympian swimmer, has ADHD, but his mother worked with him to build what might be perceived by some as negative into something very positive, swimming. Some individuals exhibit characteristics of obsessive compulsive disorder. This may be viewed negatively because the individual can sometimes get lost in everything being done perfectly. On the other hand, this can be viewed positively because the individual will always meet deadlines, and when a task is done, it is done well.

Lopez (2012) reports that engagement is high when a teacher pays attention to and develops the strengths of students, and as a result, the teacher can see the benefits of increased student engagement. Where schools engage in efforts to publicize strengths both within and outside the school, they then further increased engagement. Lopez recommends conducting a strengths profile of each student using a tool that assists in identifying skills and knowledge of the students and responding to the positive experiences with genuine excitement.

The Individuals With Disabilities Education Act (IDEA) 2004 requires that the strengths of students who are in special education are to be identified and utilized in developing the individualized plan for the student. While we provide special education to remediate and compensate for the areas in which the student is struggling, we must also look at what the student does well because we can then build from the strengths. In the individualized education program (IEP) meeting, we provide hope to the parent and to the student when we focus on all of his or her accomplishments and strengths.

While we need to work to remediate the weaknesses of the students with whom we work, we also need to build on strengths of students, and in doing so, we promote the student's belief in what he or she is able to do rather than what he or she can't do. A comprehensive intervention plan that focuses on both the strengths and deficit areas is needed.

We must identify the students' strengths by observations, parent interviews, student interviews, and strength-based assessment tools.

At the keynote banquet speech at the Learning Disabilities Association of America Convention in Anaheim California, on Friday, February 21, 2014, John Rodriquez identified himself as an individual with dyslexia and talked about his failure to achieve in elementary and high school. At the age of 16, he discovered that he had a talent in ice sculpture and, for the next several years, did very well in this creative endeavor, which became one of his careers. He later went to Harvard (Rodriguez, 2014).

LIVE ACTION FROM THE CLASSROOM

Mr. Ulez teaches first grade. He is an advocate of strength-based interventions, and before the school year begins, he talks with the parents of his students to find out as much as he can about their strengths. He learns that he has some students who have an art talent, some who are good at music, and some who are very strong in gross motor skills and love physical education. He is very excited that he has diverse talents in his classroom.

He establishes centers in his room where students can go when he provides them with the time, so they can do reading, writing, and math assignments that are based on their strengths. At the art center, students can draw pictures of what they have read or show the math they have done. At the music center, he allows students to write a song or listen to a math song. At the gross motor station, he allows students to do math by doing physical exercises, or they can read an assignment that tells them to do a specific exercise.

At each of the centers, he also has activities that capitalize on the culture of the students. They can read a story that incorporates their culture, they can do math story problems that incorporate culture, and they have the opportunity to write about aspects of their culture. His students love this because, throughout the day, there is time built in to visit the learning centers that capitalize on their strengths.

Mr. Landers is a high school teacher of English and is frustrated that he doesn't seem to be able to meet the needs of Jeremy, a student in his class who has Asperger's syndrome. Jeremy does not like to write, although he has an identified strength in punctuation and loves to punctuate sentences that are already written. Mr. Landers decides that he has to capitalize on what Jeremy likes to do, so he combines the Premack Principle with strength-based interventions. He talks to Jeremy and explains that he would like to capitalize on Jeremy's strengths in punctuation.

He requests that Jeremy write at least one paragraph with a minimum of three sentences when the class does independent writing. Jeremy will then be able to be an editor for other students. Other students will bring him their papers, and he will check their punctuation to make sure it is done correctly before they turn in their assignments for grading. The other students like this idea because they can have their punctuation checked before turning in an assignment, and that helps their grade. Jeremy is so pleased with what he is able to do and works to get his paragraph written, so he can proofread his classmates' punctuation. Mr. Landers then works to increase the number of sentences that Jeremy is expected to write.

WHAT THE RESEARCH SAYS

In order to accurately determine the strengths of each student, a strength-based assessment is necessary. According to Oliver, Cress, Savolainen, and Epstein (2013), there are indications that strength-based assessment is directly associated with better outcomes for students if the interventions determined are based on those strengths. There are a number of commercially based assessments based on strengths (Oliver et al., 2013). Educators learn about the strengths of the student through observations, parent interviews, child interviews, and commercially designed instruments. A focus on strengths based on assessment builds positive relationships with parents and with students.

Welborn, Huebner, and Hills (2012) found that student strength assessment as part of an evaluation was associated with positive effects for teacher expectations. An additional study with therapists found that, when those doing the therapy assessed strengths, there was a decrease in externalizing and internalizing behavior problems (Cox, 2006).

Nickerson and Fishman (2013) advocate that school personnel select the strength-based assessment that will facilitate its use in the school.

Problem-solving techniques that focus on defining a problem, analyzing and identifying the functions of the problem behavior, prioritizing needs, and developing a plan are critical and are discussed throughout this book. However, it is not enough to focus on the problems of the student. We must also focus on the strengths of the student; and for students with disabilities, IDEA mandates the identification of strengths. That discussion occurs during the IEP about the strengths of the student.

Many argue in the human services field that a focus on strengths leads to a more holistic picture of the individual (Tedeschi & Kilmer, 2005). In a study conducted by Bozic (2013), six children within the schools were studied. Using an assessment, the students were asked to identify their strengths. Significant was that the students were able to identify a number of their strengths. Once the children were assessed, the strengths were incorporated into an intervention strategy. One student was a chronic truant, and a strength-based assessment showed strength in writing. His writing was utilized to get him to come to school more frequently. The results of the study showed that, in four out of the five students where strength-based information was used to develop an action plan, there was evidence of positive change. In one case, there was no appreciable improvement. The strength-based approach can result in increased levels of engagement, positive emotions in the child, creativity within the intervention team, and changes in educators' expectations because they learned about the student's strengths (Bozic, 2013).

Nickerson and Fishman (203) stress that strength-based assessment and interventions can be utilized to promote mental health and resilience in children. Donovan and Nickerson (2007) found that, when strength-based data was added to a psycho-educational evaluation report, there were significant increases in multidisciplinary team members' expectations for a student with emotional and behavioral disorders.

Several authors call for initiatives that are designed to increase the happiness and well-being of children in school (Proctor et al., 2011; Seligman, Ernst, Gillham, Reivich, & Linkins, 2009). The question, however, of many school personnel is how to do this in an age where the importance of test scores is front and center in the mind of many.

Seligman, Steen, Park, and Peterson (2005) have demonstrated that writing down three things that went well each day and using identified top strengths in a new way each day for 1 week results in increased happiness and decreased signs of depression for 6 months.

Park and Peterson (2009) have conducted research showing that specific strengths of character are aligned with an increase in life satisfaction and fewer internalizing and externalizing behavior problems.

Peterson (2006) developed an instrument that is an inventory of strengths where individuals identify signature strengths that are traits that a person believes he or she has.

Proctor and colleagues (2011) tested one program—Strengths Gym—on the satisfaction and well-being of adolescents. The aim of this particular program is to encourage students to build on their strengths, learn new strengths, and to recognize strengths in other people. It has three levels that are used in the British school curriculum. The adolescents who participated in the program had higher levels of life satisfaction than adolescents who didn't participate in the curriculum. Positive emotions experienced from working on building character strengths and the increased life satisfaction that results can serve to form long-lasting personal resources that enable adolescents to flourish.

Brownlee and colleagues (2013) completed a review of the studies for strength- and resilience-based programs and found 11 studies that examined these practices. These authors define strengths as "the specific competencies and characteristics of the individual that are important for their overall development and well-being" (p. 436). Strengths are the student's abilities to survive adversity, minimizing mental and physical health problems, and promoting personal growth.

A great deal of work is being done in the area of positive behavioral support, positive psychology, and competence promotion, and those concepts are built on the premise that productive behavior rests in building on strengths in high-risk students. New approaches in the assessment and treatment of those students with behavioral disorders are emerging that blend strength-based perspectives with prevention, early intervention, and positive behavioral support (Farmer, Farmer, & Brooks, 2010).

Some of the original work on strength-based interventions came from Nicholas Hobbs in 1982. His work was based on an ecological perspective. We must identify the child's strengths in order to help the child adapt to the ecology. It is also based on developmental science that would say that, when a child's development is organized around strengths, the child is likely to display patterns of positive behavior (Farmer et al., 2010). Promoting behavioral interventions that bolster strengths is critical to sustain patterns of positive school adjustment (Cairns, 2000).

BASIC DIRECTIONS TO FOLLOW WHEN UTILIZING THIS INTERVENTION

We must identify the strengths of students, assist the student in identifying their strengths, and support students in utilizing their existing strengths to address the current issues they are facing. We must utilize a student's strengths to develop and expand skills.

1. To identify the strengths of the student, observe the student, interview the student and his or her parents, and interview previous teachers. Look closely at positive attributes you see in the student. Look at academic strengths of the student, even within areas where the student shows some deficits. As an example, the student may show problems in reading comprehension but can recognize words well. You can then build on that strength. The student may have difficulty in specific areas of math but is excellent in skills involving money. You can utilize that strength to build on other math problems.

2. When looking at disabilities of the student, look at the positive aspect of that disability. For example, a student with autism may have great strengths in the visual arena that can then be utilized in other areas. A student with ADHD may move around a lot. That can be an advantage to the student in some motor areas, and the student may gain skills in reading and in math if he or she is able to move around. A student with obsessive compulsive behaviors will want to meet deadlines for assignments.

3. Always build in time every day for all students to shine when they have the opportunity to use their strengths for academic work.

4. Think of as many activities as you can that result in students thinking about their strengths. Have students make collages of magazine pictures that depict their strengths. Give students a tree with roots, and they fill in the roots with their strengths because their strengths are their foundational roots and what cause them to grow. I like to have an activity at the end of the day where students draw another student's name and the student has to identify something that the student did positively that day. As a result, all students leave at the end of the day being recognized by their peers for a strength. For this activity, the teacher will have to be very specific about the importance of being sincere, and the teacher will have to model and participate in the activity. Another variation of this activity involves the teacher drawing each of the students' names out of a jar, and the teacher names a strength that he or she saw the student exhibit that day.

Mendler and Mendler (2012) recommend the creation of an "I Am Good at . . ." Board (p. 20) where students are asked to bring in a picture of them doing one activity that they are good at outside of school. Students are given an A card and a B card. On the A card, they write one thing they are good at outside of school and put the student's picture with the board. On card B, the students write something they are good at within school. The teacher then makes a large bulletin board of all the students' strengths, and then, when a student needs help with something, they can look at who is good at the task and ask that student for help (Mendler, 2012).

1. When working with students in special education, always remember to address the strengths of the student in the IEP and discuss at that meeting how you can incorporate the strengths of the student into the goals on which you are working.

2. It is fun to collect data on strength-based interventions because you can actually see a record of the difference between academic tasks that incorporate strengths and typical academic tasks. As an example, when you are doing a writing task that incorporates the student's skill in spelling or punctuation or drawing, provide a typical writing task, and record the number of sentences completed or any other measure you desire. Then provide one that incorporates the strengths of the student, and record the same information.

Another fun way that you can record data pertains to the strengths that the student is able to identify about himself. After conducting lessons about identifying strengths and modeling the identification of one's strengths, have students write them down. Have each student keep a record of their strengths. Throughout the day and week and month, continue to help the students identify their strengths, and have them add those to their records. This is great data to take to an IEP meeting or to send home with the students.

Some Sample Questions to Ask Students to Determine Their Strengths

What do you think you do best?

Would you rather write or tell a story?

Do you like to act in plays or skits?

What is your best subject in school?

Would you rather draw or sing a song or play a song on an instrument?

Do you prefer to be indoors or outdoors?

When you are in your favorite place, what do you like to do?

What do you want to learn more about?

Do you prefer to be around people or work alone?

In what way do you like to help other people?

What is your favorite thing to do at school?

What is your favorite thing to do at home?

Do you believe you are good at sports? If yes, what is your favorite sport?

Working With Parents on Identifying the Strengths of Their Children

Explain to the parents how you want to build on the strengths of their child. Give them examples of how you are doing that. When giving homework, incorporate the strengths of the child. When working with parents, gain as much information as you can about the strengths of the student. Ask the following questions:

1. What does your child do well at home?

2. How does your child help you?

3. Describe the last time your child did something positive for someone else.

4. When your child has free time, what does he or she do?

5. Does your child like to be around other people or prefer to be alone?

6. Would your child rather read or do math?

7. Would your child rather draw or sing or play an instrument?

8. Would your child rather write a story or tell a story?

Troubleshooting if the Intervention Is Not Working

1. I may not have modeled the identification of strengths for my students.

2. I may not have assessed my students' strengths thoroughly.

3. I may not have taught my students how to identify their own strengths.

4. I may not have provided enough academic activities that incorporated my students' strengths.

A Checklist to Help You Remember

✓ Do I interview the parent and the student to determine the strengths of the student?

✓ Do I observe the student enough to know what is a strength for the student?

✓ Do I build in as many opportunities as possible for the student to exhibit his or strengths?

✓ Do I point out the strengths of the student to the student himself or herself?

✓ Do I accentuate the strengths of the student with other students within the classroom?

Strategy 14

Sensory-Based Strategies

Understanding How Stimulation Impacts Performance

SENSORY INTERVENTIONS DEFINED

Students may engage in specific behaviors because they are overstimulated or under-stimulated by the environment. There may be too much noise or too many visual distractions, and the student is so overwhelmed that he or she cannot learn. The student may be on what we call *circuit overload*. A student may be overstimulated because of the feel of certain items of clothing. The student might be overstimulated because of lighting or because a worksheet is too busy, including too many details.

Students may be under-stimulated within the environment. They may be in need of movement to focus on a task, or they may need to be kept busy, and if it is too quiet they cannot work.

Sensory modulation dysfunction refers to a problem with turning sensory messages into behaviors that match the intensity and the nature of the sensory information provided (Miller, 2006). Dunn in 1999 explained that individuals with atypical sensory processing can display high or low thresholds to sensory stimulation.

Murray, Baker, Murray-Slutsky, and Paris (2009) explain that one of the functions of behavior is to communicate a sensory need. They define three types of sensory-based learners:

Sensory seekers are those individuals who use a high activity level to obtain the sensory information that they need. They require a high degree of movement, they may press too hard on their pencils, or they may be disorganized.

Underresponders are those individuals who may have poorly developed gross and fine motor skills, endurance, and strength. They basically have an under-responsive nervous system and require intense sensory input in order for them to respond.

Overresponders are those individuals who are overly sensitive to sensory stimulation and seem to appear to be triggered by almost everything in the environment. These children may overreact to being touched, do not like to get dirty, and may be visually distracted by too much on walls or in the room. They may refuse to go to the playground because there is too much distraction there.

Oftentimes we think of sensory problems with children with autism, but we should also think about sensory issues that may be present in students with ADHD and with many other children as well. As adults, we have specific sensory issues and can be easily overstimulated by too many visual distractions, or certain clothing may bother us because of the texture of it.

LIVE ACTION FROM THE CLASSROOM

Mrs. Sanchez teaches second grade, and she has always been bothered by fluorescent lighting because of the flickering and the humming sound that the lights make. Because of her own sensory needs, she has learned a lot about children's sensory needs and consults frequently with the occupational therapist in her building. This year, she has two children with autism and three students with ADHD in her class. She also has three students who are English learners. One of the children with autism is very bothered by noise, and the other child with autism is very bothered by the fluorescent lighting. The three students with ADHD are in need of a lot of movement during the day. She notes that one of her English learners is also bothered by the humming sound of the lights. Another girl who is an English learner twirls her hair frequently when required to pay attention for more than 5 minutes.

Mrs. Sanchez works together with the occupational therapist to establish a sensory-friendly classroom to not only meet the needs of the students with disabilities but also to assist some of her other students as well. She has a box of fidgets of different textures in her classroom that students can utilize when they need to play with an item. She has set the rule in her class that the students can play with the objects, but if they try to throw them or hit another student, the toys will be taken away. She also has doodle pads in her room so that students who need to doodle in order to concentrate can do so. She has purchased covers for her fluorescent lights. She also uses some lamps in her classroom so that the lighting is more pleasant to the students. In her room, she also has a rocker and a small swing. When students need to rock or swing while they are reading, they can use those items with permission. Mrs. Sanchez has also ordered a few exercise pedals that can be placed under the students' desks so that the students can pedal if they need to move their feet.

The occupational therapist also recommends that she get a few seat cushions that allow the students to wiggle in their chairs. Because her budget is limited, she purchases one seat cushion and then adapts the idea by getting large-size beach balls and inflating them slightly so that some of her students can use these as chair cushions. She has found that these items have made a big difference with her students. They allow movement that does not disrupt other students.

For her student who is bothered by the noise, she has headphones that the student can use when there is an activity where the noise level might be too high.

Mr. Alvarez teaches creative writing at the high school. He loves to write and eagerly teaches his students the art of writing. He recognizes that, when he wants to be the most creative in his own writing, he has to have a water bottle and likes to have soft music playing in the background. Mr. Alvarez allows his students to have their water bottles with them in class, so they can drink water as they write. He allows his students to listen to soft music with their iPods and headphones as long as they are not disrupting class. Because he has been up front with his students by explaining and enforcing the rules about how the iPods and the water bottles can be used while writing, he has not had problems with his students.

One of the things that Mr. Alvarez also has done is to have his students think about their own sensory needs—whether they need noise when they write, whether they write best when they are able to drink water, where they like to write, with what instruments they like to write, and what kind of lighting works best for them when they are writing. He has them write down their sensory needs and works with each of them to meet those needs when they are engaged in a writing task.

WHAT THE RESEARCH SAYS

There is some research suggesting the definitive positive effects of sensory-based interventions, and more is now being done because of the observations of many on how changing the environment to meet the sensory needs of students is making a positive difference.

In a number of schools, there are sensory rooms where there are rockers, swings, bouncing balls, and so on. Carter and Stephenson (2012) studied the use of multisensory environments in New South Wales, Australia, in special schools for students with severe disabilities. Thirty-six schools were surveyed on the advantages and drawbacks of those environments. Sensory stimulation was noted as the major benefit of the multisensory environments. The opportunity to relax and reductions in anxiety after using the multisensory environments were noted as advantages. Seventy-three percent listed the advantages of being able to focus on tasks away from other distractions, motivation to learn, and an opportunity for the student to control the environment through the use of switches.

In another study referred to in Strategy 10, sensory needs were addressed, and the reinforcement the student received met her oral sensory need. A young child engaged in inappropriate stereotypical behaviors, such as inappropriate vocalizations and spitting, that were maintained by reinforcement (Meador et al., 2007). A preference assessment was conducted to determine what the child liked. It was found that she liked to roll and catch a ball. When she would engage in this activity for 30 seconds, then she would get a piece of a donut, which was reinforcing to her. If she engaged in the inappropriate behavior during the 30 seconds, the time was reset and she got no donut. It was found also that her inappropriate behaviors were oral in nature. The donut provided an alternative form of oral sensation.

One of the characteristics of students with ASD is in the sensory area (Aspy & Grossman, 2007). These children may have sensory-based needs that require heightened sensory input or diminished sensory input (Murray et al., 2009).

Sensory Triggers That May Bother Students and What to Do

(Please note that this is not a list of every sensory trigger but some of the common ones.)

Sensory Triggers	What to Do
Fluorescent lighting	• Use natural lighting as much as possible. • Use lamps in the classroom. • Purchase covers for the fluorescent lights.
Tags in clothes	• Work with parents to cut out the tags or purchase tag-free clothes.
Bothered by noise	• Use headphones or earplugs. • Prepare students for high-noise times.
Moving hands frequently or twirling hair	• Use fidgets such as stress balls. • Allow doodling.
Moving feet	• Put pedals under the student's desk.
Need to suck on something	• Use a water bottle. • Allow students to suck on a straw. • Allow hard candy—consider sugar free.
Wiggling in chair	• Have the student sit on an exercise ball. • Have the student sit on a partially inflated beach ball.
Swinging or rocking	• Have a swing in the room. • Have a rocker in the room.
Clutter	• Keep the area around the student clear. • Keep items in their specified spaces. • Limit the amount of items on the wall.

BASIC DIRECTIONS TO FOLLOW WHEN UTILIZING THIS INTERVENTION

Everyone has specific sensory needs that impact how they learn. To create optimal learning environments, we have to address those needs.

1. Through your own observation and interviews with parents and students, and in some cases a consult or an evaluation by an occupational therapist who has specific expertise in sensory needs, determine what type of sensory problem the child is exhibiting.

2. Do an assessment of your classroom environment about whether there may be areas of concern for students with sensory-processing issues.

   a. Florescent lights may cause significant problems for some students because they do blink and they emit some noise that may be bothersome. There are a couple of actions that you can take if you have students who are bothered by these lights. There are covers you can purchase that go over these lights. Another option, which I am seeing in more classrooms, is that the teacher does not turn these lights on at all. Instead, the teacher utilizes natural lighting and also uses lamps within the classroom.

b. Too much clutter and other visual stimulation may cause problems for some students. They are easily distracted by too many items within the classroom and are unable to concentrate because of them.

c. Too much noise may cause problems for some students. The noise level can cause what I refer to as circuit overload for some students. Murray-Slutsky and Paris (2005) recommend sound-dampening adjustments such as acoustical tiles, carpeting, and vent covers.

d. While some children may like to be touched on the shoulder while they are working or as a form of reinforcement, some students do not like to be touched, and a slight action by the teacher to reinforce the student may result in a meltdown.

e. Some children are visually or auditorily distracted, so the classroom should have covered storage areas, and classroom displays should be well organized. Watch for areas and items that may be distracting, such as a fish tank motor.

f. The teacher should also monitor high-traffic areas. There is a lot of movement and noise in areas around the pencil sharpener, water fountain, teacher's desk, and trash can. Students who are visually or auditorily distracted should be seated away from these areas, and procedures for the use of these areas should be taught to the students (Minnesota Association for Children's Mental Health, 2006).

g. Classrooms should have a quiet place for students who need an area to calm down. Study carrels or desk blinders can be utilized but must be supervised by the teacher, and clear rules should be established concerning when and how these quiet areas can be used.

3. Do you have items in your classroom that can be utilized to meet the sensory needs of your students?

    a. Rockers and swings

    b. Pedals

    c. Exercise balls that students can use as an alternative to a chair

    d. Fidget toys

    e. Blank paper notepads for students who may need to doodle

    f. Study carrels

    g. Headphones

    h. A sensory area with bean bag chairs or rockers or swings so that you can give the students a break when they need it

    i. Music

4. Observe your students to see if they are overstimulated or under-stimulated.

5. Provide multiple opportunities for movement for students. Sensory seekers need multiple opportunities for movement during the day. Some teachers build in sensory breaks during the day.

6. Teach your students coping strategies for dealing with overstimulation or under-stimulation.

7. Desensitize students to specific triggers that may bother them. As an example, if a student is bothered by too much noise at all school assemblies, consider taking the student into the room before others are there and sit with the student to assure him or her while others come into the room.

8. Avoid surprises that may upset the student. Visual schedules are very important for students to prepare them for any changes in the schedule because change may cause the student to overreact.

9. Make sure that you are meeting the oral needs of the student. As an example, some students like to suck on items such as straws or hard candy. You may want to ensure that the student has a water bottle to suck on to meet an oral need and to keep the student hydrated.

10. Collect data on what the sensory triggers are for the student. Does the student need increased sensory input or decreased sensory input? Log what works best for the student. Log the triggers that will result in the students having difficulties. It is important for teachers to document what is effective and what is not.

Once you notice the triggers for the student, you can collect data on how the student performs when he or she is wearing clothes that seem to bother him or her and how he or she performs when wearing clothes that are sensory sensitive for him or her.

Working With Parents to Create a Sensory-Friendly Environment

Work with the parents to coordinate activities in the classroom. As an example, a student may be very bothered by tags in his or her clothes or certain textures in clothing. You can find this out by observing the student and by talking with the parent. If a student is not comfortable in his or her clothes and comes to school for high stakes testing days, he or she may not perform as well because he or she is bothered by the clothing. A sensory preference interview is included here that you can use to interview parents about how the child appears to learn best.

A Sensory Preference Interview With a Parent

Are there certain clothes that appear to bother your child?

Does your child respond better to a well-lit room or a dark room?

Does your child work better with noise or in a quiet environment?

Is your child bothered by loud noises?

Is your child bothered by clutter?

Does your child suck his or her thumb?

Does your child like to put objects in his or her mouth?

What kind of candy does your child like to suck on?

What kinds of behaviors have you noticed when your child is nervous?

Does your child pace?

Does your child play with objects?

Does your child twist his or her hair?

Does your child like to doodle?

Are there certain items that your child doesn't like to feel?

Does your child like to swing?

Does your child like to rock?

Troubleshooting if the Intervention Is Not Working

1. I may not have identified adequately what the sensory triggers are for the student. I may not have noticed that the student is bothered by the flickering fluorescent lights. I may not have noticed that the student's creative writing is not as good when he or can't drink water from a water bottle.

2. I may have assumed that the student's sensory needs are the same as mine, and that will not be the case. I may prefer bright sunlight and discover that one or some of my students don't like sunlight. I may prefer my room to be a certain temperature and I have students who prefer a warmer or cooler room.

3. I may not have the necessary tools in my classroom to meet the sensory needs of my students.

4. I may not have provided adequate opportunities for my students' movement.

5. I may not have taught the students how to identify their own sensory triggers.

6. I may not have taught the students coping strategies when they are under-stimulated or overstimulated.

A Checklist to Help You Remember

✓ Do I assess the sensory needs of my students?

✓ Do I observe the student for triggers that he or she may be overstimulated or under-stimulated?

✓ Do I make my classroom sensory friendly?

✓ Do I provide many opportunities for movement?

✓ Do I determine the sensory needs of the students within my classroom? What factors overstimulate or what factors result in under-stimulation?

✓ Do I record in the student records what the sensory needs are for my students?

✓ Do I work with the parents to determine and to meet the student's sensory needs?

Strategy 15

Student Self-Monitoring

Teaching Independence by
Having Students Monitor
Their Own Behavior

SELF-MONITORING DEFINED

Self-monitoring refers to the process where the student has ownership in his or her behavior and academic progress and monitors the behavior himself or herself so that he or she is able to observe progress. Another term used is *self-regulation*. Self-monitoring is a metacognitive strategy designed to teach students to actively think about their situation or actions, evaluate their actions, and then determine a course of future action (Menzies, Lane, & Lee, 2009).

These interventions begin with the identification of a target behavior for the student to monitor, such as time on task or work accuracy. Students are then taught to discriminate between the occurrence and nonoccurrence of the behavior (DuPaul, Laracy, & Gormley, 2013). Students are then taught to record the occurrence or nonoccurrence of the behavior when prompted by a timer or some other type of audio reminder. Students are given a chart where they can record their own behavior. The teacher develops a reinforcement system for appropriate behavior.

One of the big advantages of self-monitoring is that students see first-hand the progress they are making in relationship to themselves rather than competing with other students.

Besides charting students' behavior, students can also graph the number of spelling words they have learned or the number of words they are able to read or the number of multiplication tables they have mastered. There is no end to the progress that students can monitor, and students feel a sense of accomplishment when they see that they are making gains.

Students can also be taught how to manage academic tasks through a variety of checklists, from proofreading checklists to homework checklists to lists of things to do.

Self-monitoring can be utilized for many types of behavior including writing quality or quantity, math skills, engaged time, on-task behavior, social behaviors, and aggressive behaviors (Patton, Jolivette, & Ramsey, 2006).

Hirsch, Ennis, and McDaniel (2013) encourage student self-graphing that can help relieve some teacher responsibilities in the collection of data, and it can be used in conjunction with academic, behavioral, and social interventions. They provide several examples, including having students read aloud for 1 minute and then the student records the number of words read correctly on a graph or a student can record the frequency of times that he or she raises her hand and waits to be acknowledged.

Graphing can increase student motivation. By adding self-graphing to self-monitoring, students are able to get visual feedback on their progress over time. It can also develop graphing and analysis of data skills on the part of the student. Students can set goals to achieve and then work toward achievement of those goals and visually see their progress.

LIVE ACTION FROM THE CLASSROOM

Mr. Corydon is an elementary teacher of third graders, and his goal is to create independent learners in his class, so he utilizes a number of self-monitoring strategies. He provides proofreading checklists for all his students. Before they turn in any assignment, they are required to complete a small 3-inch by 5-inch card that asks them to check off whether they have put their names on their papers, whether they have completed all questions, whether they have used correct punctuation, and whether they have used correct spelling. When they turn in the assignment, they also have to turn in the proofreading checklist, and the teacher reviews it and the assignment. If there are any discrepancies, the teacher holds a brief, private conference with the student. He finds that, if the students know he is going to hold them accountable for completing the proofreading checklist correctly, they are likely to take it seriously.

Currently Mr. Corydon is also working with a student, Juan, who is easily distracted and is currently off task about 80 percent of the time in all of his academic subjects. Juan is always very busy watching what other students are doing and has difficulty concentrating in class. He does not complete assignments because he is not attending to the task at hand. Mr. Corydon praises Juan when he is on task, and that has improved his on-task behavior, but Juan still needs help. Mr. Corydon has assessed Juan's educational levels and finds that Juan is able to read and do math above grade level if he could concentrate.

Mr. Corydon meets with Juan and his mother and explains that he wants to work with Juan to improve his ability to do his assignments. Mr. Corydon explains that he wants to work with Juan to monitor his own on-task behavior and asks Juan whether there is something for which Juan would like to work. Juan's favorite activity is collecting baseball cards. Mr. Corydon explains that he is going to give Juan a sheet that breaks the day down into 5-minute segments, and Juan will be responsible for monitoring whether he has been on task for the 5 minutes when the vibrating timer goes off. When Juan gets five checkmarks on his card, he will get a letter for the baseball card—for example, the first time he gets five checkmarks, he will get a letter *b* and be complimented by Mr. Corydon. The next time he gets five checkmarks, he will get the letter *a*. After the next 5 minutes, he will get the letter *s* until he has the complete word, *baseball*. He then will get a baseball card. At the beginning, Mr. Corydon observes whether Juan is accurately reflecting whether he is on task for the 5-minute periods of time. In 2 weeks, Mr. Corydon is noticing that Juan is now on task about 80 percent of the time. Juan is doing well, is pleased with himself, and likes getting the baseball cards. After 2 weeks, Mr. Corydon explains that the time interval will be 10 minutes. Mr. Corydon gradually increases the time that Juan has to wait before he can give himself a check mark. At the end of each day, Mr.Corydon has Juan make a graph of how much time he was on task, and Juan takes his graph home each day to show his mother how he is doing. Mr. Corydon is excited because he has great data collected and it is shared with the mother, who is also as pleased as Mr. Corydon and Juan are.

Mr. Jonesboro has a female student, Jessica, in his high school algebra class. He has noticed that she pulls her hair when she is in his class, and he is seeing that her hair is thinning. He is not sure what he should do about this. He wants to help her but doesn't want to single her out. He talks with his colleagues who also have Jessica in class, and they have noticed the same behavior and are worried about her. They also don't know what to do. One of the other teachers has tried to talk to Jessica, but she started crying, and the teacher backed off, not wanting to put any pressure on Jessica.

Several of her teachers decide to get together and talk with the school social worker. The school social worker has been seeing Jessica but did not know that she was pulling her hair in class to the extent that she is. Jessica has a great deal of anxiety about her home situation but wants to quit pulling her hair because she is worried that her hair is getting thinner. The social worker asks the teachers for their cooperation in setting up a self-monitoring system. At the beginning of each day, Jessica will meet with the school social worker and get a self-monitoring sheet that will be divided into 15-minute periods of time. Jessica will be given a timer that vibrates every 15 minutes. Each period of time that Jessica has not pulled her hair, Jessica will leave the sheet that has the times on it blank. Her goal is to decrease the number of checks that she has. The teachers periodically ask Jessica how things are going and try to actively engage her in classes. They don't call attention to her hair pulling. At the end of each day, Jessica checks back in with the social worker to see how many checks she has. They work together to then keep a spreadsheet of how Jessica is doing. Mr. Jonesboro notices a decrease in her hair pulling, and the faculty meets periodically to see how Jessica is doing.

WHAT THE RESEARCH SAYS

Self-monitoring and regulation interventions have been associated with moderate to large effect sizes when attempting to increase on-task behavior and improving academic performance (DuPaul et al., 2013; Reid, Trout, & Schartz, 2005). There is some research (Harris, Friedlander, Saddler, Frizzelle, & Graham, 2005) that, for students with learning disabilities, when they monitor their academic performance, there are gains in both on-task behavior and academic performance.

Hodge, Riccomini, Buford, and Herbst (2006) found that self-monitoring during independent seatwork can improve accuracy in math computation skills. Self-management interventions help students with emotional and behavioral disorders practice appropriate academic behavior and learn the management skills that they don't currently have. Students who use these techniques for academic skills have shown achievement gains and a sense of satisfaction with their work (Farley, Torres, Wailehua, & Cook, 2012).

Hampshire, Butera, and Bellini (2011) used a homework checklist as a way for a student to manage his completion of his homework assignments. The checklist required the student to review homework rules, write assignments on the blank lines, bring to his mom when finished, make corrections, and then bring back to his mom. Part of the process was working with the parent. The student improved homework accuracy and completion after the introduction of the self-management system and parent participation.

Self-monitoring involves self-observation and self-recording and has been found to be appropriate for assisting students who have difficulties with on-task behaviors such as seatwork.

A number of studies (Menzies et al., 2009) show that self-monitoring is effective for students in a variety of settings and different academic content areas. It also can be used with other metacognitive strategies such as goal setting.

It has been found that, in some cases, one's awareness and counting of target behaviors serves as a useful intervention in itself (McDougall, 1998). It also has been shown that self-monitoring strategies contribute to the long-term stability of appropriate social responses of students who have difficulty reading social situations (Gable & Hendrickson, 2000).

Ryan, Pierce, and Mooney (2008) found a strong evidence base for self-monitoring at both the elementary and secondary levels.

Our ultimate goal should be for our students to manage their own behavior. Successful students are able to determine how to monitor their own behavior. Students who struggle are unable to determine what they need to do themselves to change their behavior.

Menzies and colleagues (2009) have shown that self-monitoring is a two-stage process that requires observing and recording. The students must be able to determine if they engaged in the target behavior or if they did not. Then they have to record themselves, which is an important feature of the target behavior. In order for self-monitoring to be successful, the student must understand what behavior is expected, and the student must be able to perform the behavior. Educators would only use self-monitoring for a target behavior that the student is capable of performing. If it is an inappropriate behavior, the student must be able to control the behavior. If the student engages in a high degree of hitting, the student may not be able to control the behavior, and a function-based intervention may be more appropriate to get the behavior in control before self-monitoring is utilized.

If the teacher wants the student to monitor his or her own behavior, that behavior has to occur frequently enough so that the student sees progress. If the teacher wants the student to monitor an academic skill, the student must be able to make progress. The behavior must also be easily observed by the student.

Self-monitoring is reported to be the most widely implemented self-management tool for students with emotional and behavioral disorders. Self-evaluation is embedded in the self-monitoring process (Niesyn, 2009).

McQuillan and DuPaul (1996) conducted a study that found that 66 percent of students with emotional behavioral disorders responded better to self-management strategies than interventions controlled by the teachers. Reid and colleagues (2005) found that self-management can produce improvements in academic productivity, on-task behaviors, and reduction of inappropriate behavior.

Daly and Ranalli (2003) found that self-monitoring promotes generalization of appropriate behavior in other environments and increases student independence by making students responsible for their own behavior, is inexpensive, can be used with a variety of behaviors, and can be utilized with students with a variety of ability levels.

Vanderbilt (2005) provided a sample self-monitoring chart that could be utilized with students that, at assigned intervals, simply checked whether they were doing their work, yes, or not doing their work, no. The easier the self-monitoring process, the more likely that the student will understand it and be able to complete the process.

BASIC DIRECTIONS TO FOLLOW WHEN UTILIZING THIS INTERVENTION

When establishing any self-monitoring system, it is critical to individualize the process based on the needs of the student. Some students may need to monitor their behavior, and others may need to monitor their progress in an academic area.

1. Assess the needs of the student to determine what type of self-monitoring system is needed.

2. Identify and define the behavior or the skill of concern in operational terms. Remember that the behavior or skill should be measurable, observable, and objective.

3. Determine criteria for mastery, and define that criteria based on baseline data.

4. Design a form that is simple for the student to utilize.

Make sure that the system and form are developmentally appropriate for the student. For instance, when first beginning a self-monitoring system, the teacher may want to build in short intervals. With a young child or a child with delayed developmental skills, you may want to record the behavior at hand every 5 minutes and then gradually increase the time for which the student monitors his or her own behavior.

5. Teach the student how to utilize the form that is being used. Give the student an example of one recording. You will probably want to assist the student in the beginning and then gradually fade out your assistance.

6. Teach the student what is appropriate behavior and what is inappropriate behavior if you are charting behavior. Give the students examples of each type of behavior. Utilize picture cues when explaining the desired behavior.

7. Design a reinforcement system based on what is rewarding for the student. Praise the student for progress and for using the self-monitoring system.

8. Monitor frequently to determine how the process is working.

9. When a student is utilizing the system effectively, you can begin to fade out the process by having the student monitor at less frequent intervals. Vanderbilt (2005) provided an example of fading a monitoring plan. At the beginning, the student would be monitoring on-task behavior every 5 minutes, then as the student made progress, the student would monitor the behavior every 10 minutes, then the student would monitor the behavior every 15 minutes, and so on.

10. Design a way to provide frequent feedback to the student.

11. Collecting data on a self-monitoring system is easier than some other types of data collection because the student is collecting the data for you with your monitoring of how the system is progressing. You have a record of how the student did at the beginning of the self-monitoring system and a record of how the student is doing along the way.

Working With the Parent on the Use of a Self-Monitoring System

Explain to the parent the specific type of self-monitoring system that you are utilizing with the student. Explain to the parent why you are using such a system to encourage the child's independence. Ask the parents whether they would like you to help them establish a self-monitoring system for use at home.

(Continued)

(Continued)

When giving homework assignments, build in self-monitoring systems such as a proofreading checklist—for example, have I put my name on my paper, have I checked to make sure I have answered all the questions, did I follow directions. You can use other questions that are appropriate for the nature of the assignment. The critical element is to have students self-monitor their work when they are completing homework and to show the parent how you are encouraging independence.

Sample Homework Checklist

Ask myself this question:	Yes	No
Have I reviewed my homework directions?		
Have I completed all assignments? Have I taken the completed assignments to Mom or Dad to check?		
Have I made any corrections that need to be made?		
Have I had Mom or Dad review again?		
Have I returned the homework to school?		
Have I given the homework to the teacher?		

Sample Proofreading Checklist

Answer these questions after completing the assignment:	Yes	No
Did I put my name on my paper?		
Did I read and follow the directions?		
Have I answered all the questions?		
Have I used correct punctuation?		
Have I used correct spelling?		

(A self-monitoring checklist can be used every 10 minutes or every 20 minutes depending on the student.)

When the timer goes off, I need to answer this question:	Yes	No
Was I working on the expected task?		

Troubleshooting if the Intervention Is Not Working

1. The self-management system I chose may be too difficult for the student to complete. The simpler, the better.

2. I may not have thoroughly taught the student the appropriate behavior and explained the inappropriate behavior or the specific academic skill I am targeting.

3. The self-management system could be appropriate, but I have failed to adequately explain it to the student and have not provided enough examples for the student to complete.

4. I may not have provided needed visual cues for the desired behavior that I am seeking.

5. The student may not be motivated to complete the self-management system because the reinforcement for doing so is not adequate.

6. I may have failed to adequately assess the student's needs.

7. I may not have communicated with the parents about the self-monitoring system, and the parents are not supporting the system and may be conveying their lack of support to their child.

8. I may not be monitoring the system together with the student and may not be providing adequate feedback.

A Checklist to Help You Remember

✓ Do I assess the student and his or her needs to determine which type of self-management system is needed?

✓ Do I design a simple self-management system that I know the student will be able to complete?

✓ Do I give multiple examples of the desired targeted behaviors?

✓ Do I thoroughly explain the self-management process to the student?

✓ Do I provide multiple cues to the student at the beginning of the process to ensure that the student is able to complete the self-monitoring system?

✓ Do I monitor that the system is working for the student?

✓ Do I reinforce the student for completing the self-monitoring system?

✓ Do I involve the parents in the process?

✓ Do I periodically review the progress the student is making as he or she is utilizing the self-monitoring system?

Conclusion

Did one of the interventions you read about in this book give you an aha moment about what might work with an individual student? The purpose of this book was to give you a myriad of management strategies that might fit the needs of the student who presents challenging behaviors that you currently have or will have in class.

With today's focus on academic achievement and the increase in children with behavioral concerns, we need to utilize all the positive and supportive strategies that we have to ensure that students are successful in the classroom. Many of the strategies that we utilize to improve student behavior can be utilized to increase academic skills.

This book has focused on 15 of the behavior management strategies that I have found to make not only a difference in behavior but also in academics. From the case studies, you have been provided step-by-step procedures that have been outlined; it is hoped that you have gained a repertoire of effective tools that you can utilize in your classroom.

No one intervention will be effective for all students. You know your students best and will assess their needs thoroughly before deciding which of the interventions will work and which may not. You will collaborate with peers and parents to determine the most appropriate strategies.

Throughout the book, you have noticed that some of the case study examples have incorporated more than one intervention, which is recommended when possible. Some readers may not be comfortable using some of the interventions, and it is important to remember that the tools you use must be a fit for the student and a fit for the teacher.

Recognizing that there may be some problems you face when you implement certain interventions, there are troubleshooting sections to help you determine what you might want to do when a strategy is not working for a student.

Good teachers are lifelong learners. We never have all the answers, so we need to study the interventions, study the needs of the students with whom we work, collaborate with others, and make decisions about what approach or approaches we use. Evaluation of the strategies is ongoing, and good teachers study what is working, what isn't, and what can be done differently. They seek assistance from their colleagues for additional ideas and for moral support. They learn as much as possible about what worked with previous teachers in working with students, and they share their ideas with others.

Teachers today are under pressure to utilize evidence-based interventions. These interventions have a long history of success with students, and the evidence that supports their use is included in each chapter.

As you move forward to create classrooms designed for academic and behavioral success, recognize the importance of positive behavior management strategies. Your skills in assessing students and choosing the interventions that have been utilized for many years and that are based on the specific needs of the students will make your classroom a place where students want to be and are able to experience success.

References

Allday, R., Hinkson-Lee, Hudson, T., Neilsen-Gatti, S., Kleinke, A., & Russel, C. (2012). Training general educators to increase behavior-specific praise: Effects on students with EBD. *Behavioral Disorders, 37*(2), 87–98.

Alter, P., Walker, J., & Landers, E. (2013). Teachers' perceptions of students' challenging behavior and the impact of teacher demographics. *Education and Treatment of Children, 36*(4), 51–69.

Anderson, C., Horowitz, L., & French, R. (1983). Peer rejection and loneliness in people. *Journal of Personality and Social Psychology, 45*, 127–136.

Anderson, L., Evertson, C., & Brophy, J. (1979). An experimental study of effective teaching in first grade reading groups. *Elementary School Journal, 79*, 193–223.

Aspy, R., & Grossman, B. (2007). *The Ziggurat model: A framework for designing comprehensive interventions for individuals with high-functioning autism and Asperger syndrome.* Shawnee Mission, KS: Autism Asperger Publishing Company.

Association for Supervision and Curriculum Development (ASCD). (2013). Targeting feedback to support self-regulation. *ASCD Education Update, 55*(12), 3.

Azrin, N., Vinas, V., & Ehle, C. (2007). Physical activity as reinforcement for classroom calmness of ADHD children: A preliminary study. *Child and Family Behavior Therapy, 29*(2),1–8.

Baker, M., Koegel, R., & Koegel, L. (1998). Increasing the social behavior of young children with autism using their obsessive behaviors. *Journal of the Association for Persons With Severe Handicaps, 23*, 300–308.

Banda, D., Matuszny, R., & Therrien, W. (2009). Enhancing motivation to complete math tasks using the high-preference strategy. *Intervention in School and Clinic, 44*, 146–150.

Barbetta, P., Norona, K., & Bicard, D. (2005). Classroom behavior management: A dozen common mistakes and what to do instead. *Preventing School Failure, 49*(3), 11–19.

Blood, E. (2010). Effects of student response systems on participation and learning of students with emotional and behavioral disorders. *Behavioral Disorders, 35*(3), 214–228.

Bozic, N. (2013). Developing a strength-based approach to educational psychology practice: A multiple case study. *Educational and Child Psychology, 30*(4), 18–29.

Brekelmans, M. (1989). *Interpersonal teacher behavior in the classroom.* Utrecht, The Netherlands: W.C.C. (in Dutch).

Bricker, D., Pretti-Frontczak, K., & McComas, N. (1998). *An activity-based approach to early intervention* (2nd ed.). Baltimore, MD: Brookes.

Broden, M., Bruce, C., Mitchell, M., Carter, V., & Hall, R. (1970). Effects of teacher attention on attending behavior of two boys at adjacent desks. *Journal of Applied Behavior Analysis, 3,* 199–203.

Brophy, J. (1981). Teacher praise: A functional analysis. *Review of Educational Research, 51,* 5–32.

Brown, J., Spencer, K., & Swift, S. (2002). A parent training programme for chronic food refusal: A case study. *British Journal of Learning Disabilities, 30*(3), 118–121.

Brownlee, K., Rawana, J., Franks, J., Harper, J., Bajwa, J., O'Brien, E., & Clarkson, A. (2013). A systematic review of strengths and resilience outcome literature relevant to children and adolescents. *Child Adolescent Social Work Journal, 30,* 435–459.

Brummelman, E. (2014). [Association for Psychological Services news release] *HealthDay,* January 2, 2014. Retrieved from http://wwwhealthday.com

Bryan, T. (1998). Social competence of students with learning disabilities. In B. Wong (Ed.), *Learning about learning disabilities* (2nd ed., pp. 237–275). San Diego, CA: Academic Press.

Burns, M., Ardoin, S., Parker, D., Hodgson, J., Klingbeil, D., & Scholin, S. (2009). Interspersal technique and behavioral momentum for reading word lists. *School Psychology Review, 38*(3), 428–434.

Cairns, R. (2000). Developmental science: Three audacious implications. In L. Bergman, R. Cairns, L. Nilsson, & L. Nystedt (Eds.), *Developmental science and the holistic approach* (pp. 49–62). Mahwah, NJ: Erlbaum.

Campbell, A., & Tincani, M. (2011). The power card strategy: Strength-based intervention to increase direction following of children with autism spectrum disorder. *Journal of Positive Behavior Interventions, 13*(4), 240–249.

Cannella, H., O'Reilly, M., & Lancioni, G. (2005). Choice and preference assessment research with people with severe to profound developmental disabilities: A review of the literature. *Research in Developmental Disabilities, 26,* 1–15.

Cannela-Malone, H., Sabielny, L., Jimenez, E., & Miller, M. (2013). Pick one! Conducting preference assessments with students with significant disabilities. *Teaching Exceptional Children, 45*(6), 16–23.

Carlile, K., Kelly, A., Reeve, S., Reeve, K., & DeBar, R. (2013). Using activity schedules on the iPod touch to teach leisure skills to children with autism. *Education and Treatment of Children, 36*(2), 1–22.

Carter, M., & Stephenson, J. (2012). The use of multi-sensory environments in schools serving children with severe disabilities. *Journal of Developmental and Physical Disabilities, 24*(1), 95–109.

Cheney, D., Cumming, T., & Slemrod, T. (2013). Secondary education and promising practices for students with emotional/behavioral disorders. In H. Walker & F. Gresham (Eds.), *Handbook of evidence-based practices for emotional and behavioral disorders: Applications in schools* (pp. 344–356). New York: Guilford.

Christle, C., & Schuster, J. (2003). The effects of using response cards on student participation, academic achievement, and on-task behavior during whole-class, math instruction. *Journal of Behavioral Education, 12*(3), 147–165.

Cipani, E., & Spooner, F. (1997). Treating problem behaviors maintained by negative reinforcement. *Research in Developmental Disabilities, 18,* 329–342.

Conroy, M., Asmus, J., Ladwig, C., Sellers, J., & Valcante, G. (2004). The effects of proximity on the classroom behaviors of students with autism in general education settings. *Behavioral Disorders, 29*, 119–129.

Conroy, M., Sutherland, K., Snyder, A., Al-Hendawi, M., & Vo, A. (2009). Creating a positive classroom atmosphere: Teachers' use of effective praise and feedback. *Beyond Behavior, 18*(2), 18–26.

Cortez, E., & Malian, I. (2013). A corrective teaching approach to replace undesired behaviors in students with emotional and behavioral disorders. *Beyond Behavior, 22*(3), 54–59.

Council for Exceptional Children. (1987). *Academy for effective instruction: Working with mildly handicapped students.* Reston, VA: Author.

Cox, K. F. (2006). Investigating the impact of strength-based assessment in youth with emotional or behavioural disorders. *Journal of Child and Family Studies, 15*, 287–301.

Daly, P., & Ranalli, P. (2003). Using countoons to teach self-monitoring skills. *Teaching Exceptional Children, 35*(5), 30–35.

DePry, R., & Sugai, G. (2002). The effect of active supervision and pre-correction on minor behavioral incidents in a sixth grade general education classroom. *Journal of Behavioral Education, 11*, 255–267.

DiCarlo, C., Baumgartner, J., Stephens, A., & Pierce, S. (2013). Using structured choice to increase child engagement in low-preference centres. *Early Child Development and Care, 183*(1), 109–124.

Donovan, S., & Nickerson, A. (2007). Strength-based versus traditional social-emotional reports: Impact on multidisciplinary team members' perceptions. *Behavioral Disorders, 32*, 228–237.

Duchaine, E., Green, K., & Jolivette, K. (2011). Using response cards as a class-wide intervention to decrease challenging behavior. *Beyond Behavior, 20*(1), 3–10.

Ducharme, J., & Worling, D. (1994). Behavioral momentum makes noncompliance "fade to black." *Journal of Applied Behavior Analysis, 27*, 639–647.

Dunlap, G., dePerczel, M., Clarke, S., Wilson, D., Wright, S., White, R., et al. (1994). Choice making to promote adaptive behavior for students with emotional and behavioral challenges. *Journal of Applied Behavior Analysis, 27*, 505–518.

Dunn, W. (1999). *Sensory profile.* San Antonio, TX: Psychological Corporation.

DuPaul, G., Laracy, S., & Gormley, M. (2013). Interventions for students with attention-deficit/hyperactivity disorder: School and home contexts. In H. Walker & F. Gresham (Eds.), *Handbook of evidence-based practices for emotional and behavioral disorders* (pp. 292–306). New York: Guilford.

Epstein, M., Atkins, M., Cullinan, D., Kutash, K., & Weaver, R. (2008). *Reducing behavior problems in the elementary school classroom: A practice guide* (NCEE #2008–012). Washington, DC: National Center for Education Evaluation and Regional Assistance.

Etscheidt, S., Stainback, S., & Stainback, W. (1984). The effectiveness of teacher proximity as an initial technique of helping pupils control their behavior. *The Pointer, 28*, 33–35.

Farley, C., Torres, C., Wailehua, C., & Cook, L. (2012). Evidence-based practices for students with emotional and behavioral disorders: Improving academic achievement. *Beyond Behavior, 21*(2), 37–43.

Farmer, T., Farmer, E., & Brooks, D. (2010). Recasting the ecological and developmental roots of intervention for students with emotional and behavior problems: The promise of strength-based perspectives. *Exceptionality: A Special Education Journal, 18*(2), 53–57.

Fifer, F. (1986). Effective classroom management. *Academic Therapy, 21,* 401–410.

Fry, P. (1983). Process measures of problem and non-problem children's classroom behavior: The influence of teacher behavior variables. *British Journal of Educational Psychology, 53,* 79–88.

Gable, R., & Hendrickson, J. (2000). Strategies for maintaining positive behavior change stemming from functional behavioral assessment in schools. *Education and Treatment of Children, 23,* 286–297.

Gagnon, E. (2001). *Power cards: Using special interests to motivate children and youth with Asperger syndrome and autism.* Shawnee Mission, KS: Autism Asperger.

George, C. (2010). Effects of response cards on performance and participation in social studies for middle school students with emotional and behavioral disorders. *Behavioral Disorders, 35*(3), 200–2013.

Gongola, L., & Daddario, R. (2010). A practitioner's guide to implementing a differential reinforcement of other behaviors procedure. *Teaching Exceptional Children, 42*(6),14–20.

Green, K., Mays, N., & Jolivette, K. (2011). Making choices: A proactive way to improve behaviors for young children with challenging behaviors. *Beyond Behavior, 20*(1), 25–31.

Gunter, P., Countinho, M., & Cade, T. (2002). Classroom factors linked with academic gains among students with emotional and behavioral problems. *Preventing School Failure, 46,* 126–132.

Gunter, P., Shores, R., Jack, S., Denny, R., & DePaepe, P. (1994). A case study of the effects of altering instructional interactions on the disruptive behavior of a child identified with severe behavior disorders. *Education and Treatment of Children, 17,* 435–445.

Gunter, P., Shores, R., Jack, S., Rasmussen, S., & Flowers, J. (1995). On the move: Using teacher/student proximity to improve students' behavior. *Teaching Exceptional Children, 28,* 12–16.

Hall, R., Panyan, M., Rabon, D., & Broden, M. (1968). Instructing beginning teachers in reinforcement procedures which improve classroom control. *Journal of Applied Behavior Analysis, 1,* 315–322.

Hallahan, D., Gajar, A., Cohen, S., & Tarver, S. (1978). Selective attention and locus of control in learning disabled and normal children. *Journal of Learning Disabilities, 27,* 144–154.

Hampshire, P., & Hourcade, J. (2014). Teaching play skills to children with autism using visually structured tasks. *Teaching Exceptional Children, 46*(3), 26–31.

Hampshire, P., Butera, G., & Bellini, S. (2011). Self-management and parents as interventionists: Improving homework performance in middle school students with disabilities. *Beyond Behavior, 21*(1), 28–35.

Hansen, J. (2010). Teaching without talking. *Kappan, 92*(1), 35–40.

Harlacher, J., Roberts, N., & Merrell, K. (2006). Classwide interventions for students for students with ADHD. *Teaching Exceptional Children, 39*(2), 6–12.

Harris, K., Friedlander, B., Saddler, B., Frizelle, R., & Graham, S. (2005). Self-monitoring of attention versus self-monitoring of academic performance: Effects among students with ADHD in the general education classroom. *Journal of Special Education, 39*(3), 145–156.

Haydon, T., Borders, C., Embury, D., & Clarke, L. (2009). Using effective instructional delivery as a classwide management tool. *Beyond Behavior, 18*(2), 12–17.

Haydon, T., Conroy, M., Sindelar, P., Scott, T., Barber, B., & Orlando, A. (2010). A comparison of three types of opportunities to respond on student academic and social behaviors. *Journal of Emotional and Behavioral Disorders, 18*, 27–40.

Haydon, T., MacSuga-Gage, Simonsen, B., & Hawkins, R. (2012). Opportunities to respond: A key component of effective instruction. *Beyond Behavior, 22*(1), 23–31.

Hershfeldt, P., Rosenberg, M., & Bradshaw, C. (2010). Function-based thinking: A systematic way of thinking about function and its role in changing student behavior problems. *Beyond Behavior, 19*(3), 12–21.

Heward, W. (2009). *Exceptional children: An introduction to special education* (9th ed.). Upper Saddle River, NJ: Merrill/Prentice-Hall.

Himmele, P., & Himmele, W. (2011). *Total participation techniques: Making every student an active learner.* Alexandria, VA: ASCD.

Hirsch, S., Ennis, R., & McDaniel, S. (2013). Student self-graphing as a strategy to increase teacher effectiveness and student motivation. *Beyond Behavior, 22*(3), 31–39.

Hobbs, N. (1982). *The troubled and troubling child.* San Francisco, CA: Jossey-Bass.

Hodge, J., Riccomini, P., Buford, R., & Herbst, M. (2006). A review of instructional interventions in mathematics for students with emotional and behavioral disorders. *Behavioral Disorders 31*(3), 297–311.

Horner, R., Sugai, G., & Anderson, C. (2010). Examining the evidence base for school-wide positive behavior support. *Focus on Exceptional Children, 42*(8), 1–16.

Houtz, J., & Feldhusen, J. (1976). The modification of fourth graders' problem solving abilities. *Journal of Psychology, 93*, 229–237.

Individuals With Disabilities Education Improvement Act. Public Law Number 108-446 (2004).

Iovanonne, R., Anderson, C., & Scott, T. (2013). Power and control: Useful functions or explanatory fictions? *Beyond Behavior, 22*(2), 3–6.

Jaspers, K., Skinner, C., Williams, R., & Suecker, L. (2007). Effects of problem order on accuracy, preference, and choice of multiplication assignments. *The Behavior Analyst, 8*(3), 347–359.

Jitendra, A., Griffin, C., McGoey, K., Gardill, M., Bhat, P., & Riley, T. (1998). Effects of mathematical word problem solving by students at risk or with mild disabilities. *Journal of Educational Research, 91*, 341–355.

Johns, B. (2011). *401 practical adaptations for every classroom.* Thousand Oaks, CA: Corwin.

Kendrick, A., Hernandez-Reif, M., Hudson, C., Jeon, H., & Horton, C. (2012). Coding group behaviors for preschool children in the playground and the effects of teachers' proximity on preschool children's playground behaviors. *Early Child Development and Care, 182*(6), 665–682.

Kern, L., Bambra, L., & Fogt, J. (2002). Classwide curricular modifications to improve the behavior of students with emotional and behavioral disorders. *Behavioral Disorders, 27*, 317–326.

Kern, L., Mantegna, M., Vorndran, C., Bailin, D., & Hilt, A. (2001). Choice of task sequence to reduce problem behaviors. *Journal of Positive Behavioral Interventions, 3*(1), 3–10.

Kern, L., & State, T. (2009). Incorporating choice and preferred activities into class-wide instruction. *Beyond Behavior, 18*(2), 3–11.

Knoff, H. (2012). *School discipline, classroom management, and student self-management: A PBS implementation guide.* Thousand Oaks, CA: Corwin.

Knox, M., Rue, H., Wildenger, L., Lamb, K., & Luiselli, J. (2012). Intervention for food selectivity in a specialized school setting: Teacher implemented prompting, reinforcement, and demand fading for an adolescent student with autism. *Education and Treatment of Children, 35*(3), 407–417.

Kodak, T., Miltenberger, R., & Romaniuk, C. (2003). A comparison of differential reinforcement and noncontingent reinforcement for the treatment of a child's multiply control problem behavior. *Behavioral Interventions, 18,* 267–278.

Koegel, R., Fredeen, R., Kim, S., Danial, J., Rubinstein, D., & Koegel, L. (2012). Using perseverative interests to improve interactions between adolescents with autism, and their typical peers in school settings. *Journal of Positive Behavior Interventions, 14*(3), 133–141.

Lambert, N., & Miller, A. (2010). The temporal stability and predictive validity of pupils' causal attributions for difficult classroom behavior. *British Journal of Educational Psychology, 80,* 599–622.

Lampi, A., Fenty, N., & Beaunae, C. (2005). Making the three ps easier: Praise, proximity, and precorrection. *Beyond Behavior, 15*(1), 8–12.

Lee, D. L. (2005). Increasing compliance: A quantitative synthesis of applied research on high-probability request sequences. *Exceptionality, 13*(3), 141–154.

Lee, D., Belfiore, P., & Budin, S. (2008) Riding the wave: Creating a momentum of school success. *Teaching Exceptional Children,* January/February, 65–70.

Lee, D., Belfiore, P., Ferko, D., Youjia, H., Carranza, M., & Hildebrand, K. (2006). Using pre and post low "p" latency to assess behavioral momentum: A preliminary investigation. *Journal of Behavioral Education, 15*(4), 203–214.

LeGray, M., Dufrene, B., Sterling-Turner, H., Olmi, D., & Bellone, K. (2010). A comparison of function-based differential reinforcement interventions for children engaging in disruptive classroom behavior. *Journal of Behavioral Education, 19,* 185–204.

Lewis, T. J., Colvin, G., & Sugai, G. (2000). The effects of precorrection and active supervision on the recess behavior of elementary school students. *Education and Treatment of Children, 23,* 109–121.

Lopez, S. (2012). Does your school build on strengths. *Kappan,* March, 70–71.

Mace, F. C., Auro, B., Oyajian, A., & Ckert, T. (1997). Effects of reinforcer quality on behavioral momentum: coordinated applied and basic research. *Journal of Applied Behavior Analysis, 30,* 1–20.

Mainhard, M., Brekelmans, M., & Wubbells, T. (2011). Coercive and supportive teacher behavior: Within-and across-lesson associations with the classroom social climate. *Learning and Instruction, 21,* 345–354.

Margolis, H., & McCabe, P. (2003). Self-efficacy: A key to improving the motivation of struggling learners. *Preventing School Failure, 47*(4), 162–169.

Matson, J., Shoemaker, M., Sipes, M., Horovitz, M., Worley, J., & Kozlowski, A. (2011). Replacement behaviors for identified functions of challenging behaviors. *Research in Developmental Disabilities, 32,* 681–684.

McBride, B., & Schwartz, I. (2003). Effects of teaching early interventionists to use discrete trials during ongoing classroom activities. *Topics in Early Childhood Special Education, 23*(1), 5–17.

McCoy, K., Mathur, S., & Czoka, A. (2010). Guidelines for creating a transition routine: Changing from one room to another. *Beyond Behavior, 19*(3), 22–29.

McCurdy, M., Skinner, C., Grantham, K., Watson, T., & Hindman, P. (2001). Increasing on-task behavior in an elementary student during mathematics seatwork by interspersing additional brief problems. *School Psychology Review, 30*(1), 23–32.

McDougall, D. (1998). Research on self-management techniques used by students with disabilities in general education settings: A descriptive review.[Electronic version]. *Remedial and Special Education, 19,* 310–320.

McIntosh, K., Herman, K., Sanford, A., McGraw, K., & Florence, K. (2004). Teaching transitions: Teaching for promoting success between lessons. *Teaching Exceptional Children, 37,* 32–38.

McKibben, S. (2014). Boys can write! *ASCD Education Update, 56*(1), 1, 6.

McNeill, K., Lizotte, D., Krajcik, J., & Marx, R. (2006). Supporting students' construction of scientific explanations by fading scaffolds in instructional materials. *The Journal of the Learning Sciences, 15*(2), 153–191.

McQuillan, K., & DuPaul, G. (1996). Classroom performance of students with serious emotional disturbance. A comparative study of evaluation methods for behavior management. *Journal of Emotional and Behavioral Disorders, 4*(3), 162–170.

Meador, S., Derby, M., McLaughlin, T., Barreto, A., & Weber, K. (2007). Using response latency within a preference assessment. *The Behavior Analyst Today, 8*(1), 63–69.

Mendler, A., & Mendler, B. (2012). *Power struggles: Successful techniques for educators* (2nd ed.). Bloomington, IN: Solution Tree.

Menzies, H., Lane, K., & Lee, J. (2009). Self-monitoring strategies for use in the classroom: A promising practice to support productive behavior for students with emotional or behavioral disorders. *Beyond Behavior, 18*(2), 27–35.

Messling, P., & Dermer, M. (2009). Increasing student's attendance at lecture and preparation for lecture by allowing students to use their notes during tests. *The Behavior Analyst Today, 10*(3–4), 381–390.

Miller, L. (2006). *Sensational kids: Hope and help for children with sensory processing disorder.* New York: Putnam.

Minnesota Association for Children's Mental Health. (2006). *An educator's guide to children's mental health.* St. Paul: Minnesota Association for Children's Mental Health.

Morgan, P. (2006). Increasing task engagement using reference or choice-making: Some behavioral and methodological factors affecting their efficacy as classroom interventions. *Remedial and Special Education, 27*(3), 176–187.

Mueller, M., Palkovic, C., & Maynard, C. (2007). Errorless learning: Review and practical application for teaching children with pervasive developmental disorders. *Psychology in the Schools, 44,* 691–700.

Murphy, C., Figueroa, M., Martin, G., Yu, C., & Figueroa, J. (2008). The use of computer-generated fading materials to teach visual-visual non-identity matching tasks. *Developmental Disabilities Bulletin, 36*(1–2), 49–66.

Murray, M., Baker, P., Murray-Slutsky, & Paris, B. (2009). Strategies for supporting the sensory-based learner. *Preventing School Failure, 53*(4), 245–251.

Murray-Slutsky, C., & Paris, B. (2005). *Is it sensory or is it behavior?* San Antonio, TX: Harcourt.

National Governors Association Center for Best Practices and Council of Chief State School Officers. (2010). *Common Core State Standards for English language arts and literacy in history/social studies, science, and technical subjects.* Washington, DC: Author.

Nickerson, A., & Fishman, C. (2013). Promoting mental health and resilience through strength-based assessment in U.S. schools. *Educational and Child Psychology, 30*(4), 7–17.

Niesyn, M. (2009). Strategies for success: Evidence-based instructional practices for students with emotional and behavioral disorders. *Preventing School Failure, 53*(4), 227–233.

Nuernberger, J., Vargo, K., & Ringdahl, J. (2013). An application of differential reinforcement of other behavior and self-monitoring to address repetitive behavior. *Journal of Developmental and Physical Disabilities, 25*, 105–117.

Okolo, C. (1992). The effects of computer-based attribution retraining on the attributions, persistence, and mathematics computation of students with learning disabilities. *Journal of Learning Disabilities, 25*, 327–334.

Oliver, R., Cress, C., Savolaien, H., & Epstein, M. (2013). Strength-based assessment issues, tolls, and practices in school-related contexts and schools in the United States and Finland. In H. Walker & F. Gresham (Eds.), *Handbook of evidence-based practices for emotional and behavioral disorders* (pp. 229–242). New York: Guilford.

Ozen, A., & Ergenekon, Y. (2011). Activity-based intervention practices in special education. *Educational Sciences: Theory and Practice, 11*(1), 359–362.

Park, C., Weber, K., & McLaughlin, T. (2007). The effects of adding, modeling, prompting and direct instruction on letter legibility for two preschool students with physical and developmental delays. *Child and Family Behavior Therapy, 29*, 13–21.

Park, K. (2007). Facilitating effective team-based functional behavioral assessments in typical school settings. *Beyond Behavior, 17*(1), 21–31.

Park, N., & Peterson, C. (2009). Strengths of character in schools. In R. Gilman, E. Huebner, & M. Furlong (Eds.), *Handbook of positive psychology in schools* (pp. 65–76). New York: Routledge.

Patton, B., Jolivette, K., & Ramsey, M. (2006). Students with emotional and behavioral disorders can manage their own behavior. *Teaching Exceptional Children, 39*(2), 14–21.

Peterson, C. (2006). *A primer in positive psychology.* New York: Oxford University Press.

Proctor, C., Tsukayama, E., Wood, A., Maltby, J., Eades, J., & Linley, P. (2011). Strengths Gym: The impact of a character strengths-based intervention on the life satisfaction and well-being of adolescents. *The Journal of Positive Psychology, 6*(5), 377–388.

Randolph, J. (2007). Meta-analysis of the research on response cards. Effects in test achievement, quiz achievement, participation, and off-task behavior. *Journal of Positive Behavioral Interventions, 9*(2), 113–128.

Raney, M. (1997). Interview with Jeff Howard. *Technos, 6*(2), 4–11.

Reeves, D. (2011). From differentiated instruction to differentiated assessment. *ASCD Whole Child Bloggers.* Retrieved from www.wholechildeducation.org

Reid, R., Trout, A., & Schartz, M. (2005). Self-regulation interventions for children with attention deficit/hyperactivity disorder. *Exceptional Children, 71*, 361–377.

Reinke, W., Lewis-Palmer, T., & Merrell, K. (2008). The classroom check-up: A classwide consultation model or increasing praise and decreasing disruptive behavior. *School Psychology Review 37*, 315–332.

Rodriguez, J. (2014). High school dropout to Harvard: My life with dyslexia. Learning Disabilities Association banquet keynote, Anaheim, CA, February, 21, 2014.

Ryan, J., Pierce, C., & Mooney, P. (2008). Evidence-based teaching strategies for students with EBD. *Beyond Behavior, 17*(3), 22–27.

Sakaki, M., & Murayama, K. (2013). Automatic ability attribution after failure: A dual process view of achievement attribution. *PLOS ONE, 8*(5), 1–4. Retrieved from www.plosone.org

Schunk, D., & Rice, J. (1993). Strategy fading and progress feedback: Effects on self-efficacy and comprehension among students. *Journal of Special Education 27*(3), 257–276.

Schwab, J., Tucci, S., & Jolivette, K. (2013). Integrating schema-based instruction and response cards for students with learning disabilities and challenging behaviors. *Beyond Behavior, 22*(3), 24–30.

Seiverling, L., Kokitus, A., & Williams, K. (2012). A clinical demonstration of a treatment package for food selectivity. *The Behavior Analyst Today, 13*(2), 11–16.

Seligman, M., Ernst, R., Gillham, J., Reivich, K., & Linkins, M. (2009). Positive education: Positive psychology and classroom interventions. *Oxford Review of Education, 35*, 293–311.

Seligman, M., Steen, T., Park, N., & Peterson, C. (2005). Positive psychology progress: Empirical validation of interventions. *American Psychologist, 60*, 410–421.

Sills-Briegel, T. (1996). Teacher-student proximity and interactions in a computer laboratory and classroom. *Clearinghouse, 70*(1), 21–23.

Simonsen, B., Fairbanks, S., Briesch, A., Myers, D., & Sugai, G. (2008). Evidence-based practices in classroom management: Considerations for research to practice. *Education and Treatment of Children, 31*, 351–380.

Singh, A., Matson, J., Mouttapa, M., Pella, R., Hill, B., & Thorson, R. (2009). A critical item analysis of the QABF: Development of a short form assessment. *Research in Developmental Disabilities, 30*, 782–792.

Skinner, C. (2002). An empirical analysis of interspersal research evidence, implications, and applications of the discrete task completion hypothesis. *Journal of School Psychology, 40*(4), 347–368.

Skinner, C., Hall-Johnson, K., Skinner, A., Cates, G., Weber, J., & Johns, G. (1999). Enhancing perceptions of mathematics assignments by increasing relative problem completion rates through the interspersal technique. *Experimental Education, 68*(1), 1–20.

Stephanou, G. (2012). Students' school performance in language and mathematics: Effects of hope on attributions, emotions and performance expectations. *International Journal of Psychological Studies, 4*(2), 93–119.

Stipek, D. J., & Daniels, D. H. (1988). Declining perceptions of competence: A consequence of changes in the child or in the educational environment? *Journal of Educational Psychology, 80*, 352–356.

Stormont, M., & Reinke, W. (2009). The importance of precorrective statements and behavior-specific praise and strategies to increase their use. *Beyond Behavior, 18*(3), 26–32.

Stowitschek, J., Laitinen, R., & Prather, T. (1999). Embedding early self-determination opportunities in curriculum for youth with developmental disabilities using natural teaching incidents. *Journal of Vocational Special Needs Education, 21,* 15–26.

Sutherland, K., Alder, N., & Gunter, P. (2003). The effect of varying rates of opportunities to respond to academic requests on the classroom behavior of students with EBD. *Journal of Emotional and Behavioral Disorders, 11*(4), 239–248.

Sutherland, K., Wehby, J., & Copeland, S. (2000). Effect of varying rates of behavior-specific praise on the on-task behavior of students with EBD. *Journal of Emotional and Behavioral Disorders, 8*(1), 2–8, 26.

Swinton, A., Kurtz-Costes, B., Rowley, S., & Okeke-Adeyanju, N. (2011). A longitudinal examination of African American adolescents' attributions about achievement outcomes. *Child Development, 82*(5), 1486–1500.

Tedeschi, R., & Kilmer, R. (2005). Assessing strengths, resilience, and growth to guide clinical interventions. *Professional Psychology: Research and Practice, 36*(3), 230.

Teeple, D., & Skinner, C. (2004). Enhancing grammar assignment perceptions by increasing assignment demands: Extending additive interspersal research to students with emotional and behavioral disorders. *Journal of Emotional and Behavioral Disorders, 12*(2), 120–127.

Turnbull, A., Turnbull, R., Erwin, E., Soodak, L., & Shogren, K. (2011). *Families, professionals, and exceptionality: Positive outcomes through partnerships and trust.* Boston: Pearson.

Van Acker, R., & Grant, S. (1996). Teacher and student behavior as a function of risk for aggression. *Education and Treatment of Children, 19*(3), 316–334.

van Amelsvoort, J. (1999). *Perspectives on instruction, motivation and self-regulation.* Unpublished doctoral dissertation. Nijmegen, the Netherlands: Katholieke Universiteit Nijmegen (in Dutch).

Vanderbilt, A. (2005). Designed for teachers: How to implement self-monitoring in the classroom. *Beyond Behavior, 15*(1), 21–24.

Vostal, B. (2011). Engaging students with behavior disorders in mathematics practice using the high-p strategy. *Beyond Behavior, 21*(1), 3–9.

Vostal, B., & Lee, D. (2011). Behavioral momentum during a continuous reading task: An exploratory study. *Journal of Behavioral Education, 20,* 163–181.

Weiner, B. (2005). Motivation from an attribution perspective and the social psychology of perceived competence. In A. Elliot & C. Dweck (Eds.), *Handbook of competence and motivation* (pp. 73–84). New York: Guilford.

Welborn, C., Huebner, E., & Hills, K. (2012). The effects of strength-based information on teachers' expectations for diverse students. *Child Indicators Research, 5,* 357–374.

Wells, A., & Axe, J. (2013). A three-tiered approach for addressing nonsuicidal self-injury in the classroom. *Beyond Behavior, 22*(2), 35–43.

Welsh, D., Bernstein, D., & Luthans, F. (1993). Application of the Premack Principle of reinforcement to the quality performance of service employees. *Journal of Organizational Behavior Management, 13*(1), 9–32.

Whitford, D., Liaupsin, C., Umbreit, J., & Ferro, j. (2013). Implementation of a single comprehensive function-based intervention across multiple classrooms for a high school student. *Education and Treatment of Children, 36*(4), 147–167.

Wiley, D., & Heitzman, A. (2001). Premacking with micro-computers. *Education, 106*(4), 462–467.

Wright, D., & Gurman, H. (1994). Positive interventions for serious behavior problems: Best practices implementing the Hughes Bill (A.B. 2586) and the positive behavioral intervention regulations. Sacramento, CA: Resources in Special Education. Retrieved from http://www.pent.ca.gov/pos/cl/str/useofreinforcement.pdf

Wubbels, T., & Brekelmans, M. (2005). Two decades of research on teacher–student relationships in class. *International Journal of Educational Research, 43,* 6–24.

Index

A SAGE Company

Corwin is committed to improving education for all learners by publishing books and other professional development resources for those serving the field of PreK–12 education. By providing practical, hands-on materials, Corwin continues to carry out the promise of its motto: **"Helping Educators Do Their Work Better."**